MW01610024

Under His H
big game. It's down to earth and touches you where
you live, play, and think. It's the kind of devotional
book that motivates you to compete in life and become
a real champion.

This sports devotional deals with the realities of
living in a fallen world with its disappointments, broken relationships, unfulfilled longings, and shattered
dreams. It meets you where you are ... preparing to go
through, in the midst of, or just coming out of one
of life's many battles. Under His Helmet offers godly
wisdom and practical insight to help you become a
champion in life.

PASTOR WM. DWIGHT MCKISSIC, SR.
Senior Pastor
Cornerstone Baptist Church, Arlington, Texas


Our sister Mrs. Melanie Garrett has written a book
that would be an inspiration to Christians and those
who are yet to become one. In this book, Melanie skill-
fully draws analogies from the game of football for
practical Christian living. The book offers immense
insight that will be of help to readers. I recommend
this book highly.

KENNEDY A. ADARKWA, PHD.
Assistant Professor, NT, Liberty Online (LUO)
Liberty University
Lynchburg, Virginia


This book is a must read, especially for those who love
and or play the game of American football. Melanie

has used her knowledge of this great American game to illustrate biblical truth in a way that captures the reader's attention from start to finish. It is inspiring yet funny. I am convinced that it has transformational qualities that will impact many lives for generations to come.

REV. CECIL CORNELIUS
Minister of Counseling and Pastoral Care
Cornerstone Baptist Church, Arlington, Texas

This book is a great evidence of the vision God has given [Melanie] to continue the powerful ways of serving and enlightening people to become all that they can be. What a great asset and playbook!

BYRON WILLIAMS
NFL Alumni-wide receiver

**BYRON WILLIAMS**
NEW YORK GIANTS

# UNDER HIS HELMET

# UNDER HIS HELMET

## A FOOTBALL DEVOTIONAL

### MELANIE GARRETT

Tate Publishing *& Enterprises*

Published by Tate Publishing & Enterprises, LLC
127 E. Trade Center Terrace | Mustang, Oklahoma 73064 USA
1.888.361.9473 | www.tatepublishing.com

Tate Publishing is committed to excellence in the publishing industry. The company reflects the philosophy established by the founders, based on Psalm 68:11,
*"The Lord gave the word and great was the company of those who published it."*

Book design copyright © 2010 by Tate Publishing, LLC. All rights reserved.
*Cover design by Rebekah Garibay*
*Cover photo by Melanie Garrett*
*Author photos by Lisa Mason Photography*
*Hair and make up by Billy Beggs, senior stylist, Salon B, Arlington, Texas*
*Interior design by Stefanie Rane*

Published in the United States of America

ISBN: 978-1-61739-174-3
1. Religion, Christian LIfe, Devotional
2. Sports & Recreation, Football
10.10.19

# **Acknowledgments**

The Bible tells us there is no such thing as a self-made man (or woman). Based on this understanding, I would be remiss if I didn't share my gratitude for the help and support of those who have invested in me and this book.

Let me start off with thanking Dr. Tate and the incredible staff at Tate Publishing. What a fabulous organization. All of the staff have been friendly, helpful, and professional.

A heartfelt thank you to Dr. Randall Bassett, Dr. Kennedy Adarkwa and Mrs. Rhonda Miller for the countless hours of proofreading my manuscript.

Wm. Dwight McKissic, senior pastor of Cornerstone Baptist Church, Arlington, Texas. Pastor, thank you for helping me to see God's vision for this book and for believing in me.

Alfred Anderson, former running back for the Minnesota Vikings; Byron Williams, former wide receiver for the New York Giants; and Larry Harris, former special teams player for the Washington Redskins. Thank you for letting me have a glimpse into the NFL by sharing some of your memories and experiences with me. I appreciate your ongoing input and feedback.

The late John Weber, former chaplain to the Dallas Cowboys. I'm thankful for his support and encouragement to finish strong the vision God has given into my care.

Billy Beggs; senior hair stylist of Salon B, Arlington, Texas. Thanks, Billy, for helping me to look as young as I feel.

Cecil Cornelius, assistant pastor, Cornerstone Baptist Church. What an awesome prayer warrior. Thank you for your continued prayerful support.

Kennedy Adarkwa, assistant professor of New Testament, Liberty University. Such an insightful and dynamic theologian. Thank you for challenging me constantly to be growing in my personal study of the Bible.

Eloise Garrett, my mother in law. Thank you for continuing to lift me up in prayer.

Lorraine Webster, my forever friend. For not knowing (or caring) that much about football, you have demonstrated your love for me in listening to me chatter on and on about this game I love so much. Thank you for your patient spirit.

The late Eva C. Bassett, my beautiful little mother. I am so grateful to you for setting the example of a loving wife and mother. (And thank you for all the spelling practice in second grade.)

The late William T. Bassett, my strong and heroic daddy. I am so grateful that you showed me what a godly man looks like. Thank you for being my first (and favorite) pastor and for leading me to know Jesus as my Savior.

Randall K. Bassett, my brilliant brother and friend. Thank you for using your awesome talent to challenge me and my writing. I am always growing because of you.

Jonathan Garrett, my precious firstborn. Your passion for evangelism has spurred me on to share Christ with all I meet. Thank you for being willing to talk football with me and constantly challenging me on my stats. Maybe I'll beat you one day.

Lydia Garrett, my gorgeous baby girl. You have consistently encouraged and believed in me. Thank you for being a good listener, as I have shared many of my ideas with you at "our" Starbucks.

Dustin Garrett, my best friend and husband of twenty-seven years. Thank you for being so giving of yourself. You have graciously deferred to me adorning our house, pets, and myself in football team attire. You have watched countless hours of football games, movies, and shows with me. But most of all, thank you for encouraging me to keep pursuing my dreams. I look forward to spending the rest of our lives together.

# Dedication

This book is lovingly dedicated to the legacy and memory of William Travis Bassett, veteran, chaplain, pastor, friend, and hero. I love and miss you, Daddy.

# Table of Contents

# Foreword

What a blessing! My good friend, Melanie Garrett, has composed a remarkable book, *Under His Helmet*. In her own words, she uniquely and simplistically compares the Christian journey to one of my favorite sports ... Football! When you consider all the struggles and disappointments that we share as players, coaches, and even fans, it is refreshing to see the way that Melanie can keep everything in perspective.

There is not anyone I have more respect for as a Christian follower and person than Melanie Garrett. She represents all that is good in her walk with Christ. God has blessed her with great leadership ability and patience. She excels in her passion to educate others about the goodness of God and his marvelous works.

As a former NFL player, I can honestly say my walk with Jesus reflects the way I played the game of football. I have always held the scripture, Philippians 4:13, close to my heart-"I can do all things through Christ who strengthens me" (NKJV). Even back then, I knew that every victory on the field was accomplished through the grace of God.

The insight from this book will lend you a true picture of Christ along with an entertaining perspective of football coming from a person who definitely admires the game. One thing I truly know about Melanie is not to say anything bad about her Dallas Cowboys.

**ALFRED ANDERSON**
Minnesota Vikings
84-91, RB

*ALFRED ANDERSON*
*MINNESOTA VIKINGS*

*THE MAKING OF*
*CHAMPIONS*

# Preface

Hello, friend.

Grab a cup of coffee, drag up a chair, and let's visit for a bit.

I've had several people ask me why I like football so much. I definitely like how it mirrors the battles and challenges of our everyday lives. But it's more than that. It might sound a tad crazy to you, but it's like my sanctuary. It's a place of refuge and worship. I can't explain it, but it's where I see God's hand at work and hear His voice the most clearly. It might not make much sense to most, but then God never does worry Himself with whether His plans meet our approval or not. He seems to delight in choosing the illogical to confuse those who think themselves too wise.

You know, I'm glad you've picked up this book. Each time you read it, I hope you will be encouraged to:

- love Christ,
- live for Him,
- trust Him to live through you,
- melt into His loving embrace,

- be ravenously hungry to be fed from His Word, and

- pass the Rock to that one who desperately needs to receive salvation.

Yours in faith and football,

**MELANIE**

# The Helmet

**S**ports equipment manufacturers have the daunting task of designing a helmet that protects the athlete from jarring hits, crushing landings, and helmet-to-helmet collisions. Have you ever looked inside an NFL helmet? There are large cushions all around. Look up. There is the center, top cushion. Some helmets are designed to add air to that cushion as an extra element for protection. Filling in the gaps are smaller pads, often made of Styrofoam. All the different forms of padding serve one purpose: to protect the head. The emphasis to provide protection is crucial. The brain is the sole organ that gives all the commands to the entire body. Without the brain, the body would not be able to function and the body would die.

God, the Master Designer of our brain, knows the importance of our mind. Our Father knows that what we do will first be generated from what we think.

"For as he thinks in his heart, so is he" (Proverbs 23:7, NKJV).

Since we will take action on what we believe, this is why it is so critical for us to protect our minds. God teaches us how in His Word. First, we must "take the helmet of salvation" (Ephesians 6:17, NKJV).

It doesn't end there. We must keep our minds safe. He tells us to, "be transformed by the renewing of your mind" (Romans 12:2).

We protect our minds by keeping them actively engaged in thinking right thoughts.

> Whatever is true, whatever is noble, whatever is right, whatever is pure, whatever is lovely, whatever is admirable—if anything is excellent or praiseworthy—think about such things (Philippians 4:8).

Before you "take the field" for the day, make sure you are *Under His Helmet.*

## Study the Playbook

**READ:** Philippians 2:5–7 (NKJV)

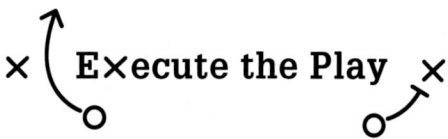

## Execute the Play

Is your "helmet" (mind) damaged by dangerous thoughts? Write them down and then throw them in the trash, where they belong. What victorious thoughts will you put in their place? Write those down and keep them where you will see them every day.

# A Different Touch

On September 19, 2005, "The Triplets" were inducted into the Cowboys Ring of Honor. Of course, I'm referring to Troy Aikman, Emmitt Smith, and Michael Irvin. Our local newspaper featured a commemorative poster of these three. It is a keepsake I will treasure.

At first, I only saw the sentiment behind the picture: the glory in this honor and the bitter sweetness of glory days gone by. But as I studied the picture more closely, I saw some interesting commonalities. Each man held the ball. Each man carried it with pride. Each man protected the ball.

At that point, the similarities stopped. It was interesting to see how differently they all handled the ball. As quarterback, Troy had a firm and commanding grasp on the ball. He held it while carefully studying where he would send it next. As the star running back, Emmitt tucked the ball into his chest and wrapped it up as if it was a priceless treasure. And as "The Playmaker," Michael cradled the ball as if it was his firstborn. Each man was a gifted athlete with impressive stats. Different positions required different skills. Three men, three different touches. Yet they all shared a common goal: victory.

Can you imagine if they had begun to criticize each other and compare the value of their talent and positions? If they had made a practice of minimizing the importance of each other's contributions, do you think the Cowboys would have enjoyed such illustrative success? It's highly doubtful. The same can be said about the church. When individuals begin to compare themselves and their respective ministries/service, they minimize their personal effectiveness and take away from their collective victory. Paul warned the Christians in Rome not to fall prey to the enemy's tactic to divide. He encouraged them to measure themselves only by God's gift of faith and to do what they were uniquely equipped to do and to do it well.

Three men, three different positions, three different styles, three sets of Super Bowl rings, three names honored, victory times three—that's the Master's touch in triplicate.

> Do not think more highly of yourself than you ought, but rather think of yourself with sober judgment, in accordance with the measure of faith God has given you. Just as each of us has one body with many members, and these members do not have the same function, so in Christ we who are many form one body, and each member belongs to all the others. We have different gifts, according to the grace given us.
>
> Romans 12:3–6

# Study the Playbook

**READ:** 1 Peter 5:6; 1 Thessalonians 5:11

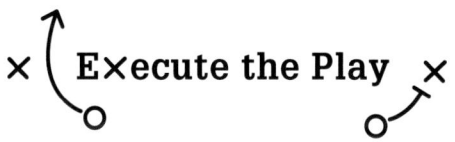

## Execute the Play

Are you struggling with jealousy towards others? Do you have a critical spirit towards people who are more successful or talented than you are? Surprise them and yourself: give them the praise they are due. Now, pray for God to continue to bless them.

_____

_____

_____

_____

_____

_____

_____

_____

_____

_____

_____

# Believe in Now

Every season, the NFL sports a promotional slogan. It is intended to inspire each athlete and team to victory (and ultimately the Super Bowl). Yet, these slogans are so broad in their appeal and applications that they work equally well in the corporate office, blue-collar job site, the classroom, or the family home. For 2008, the NFL hoped to score with the phrase, "Believe in Now."

I've wondered why the NFL felt the need to promote this philosophy. Maybe it's too easy to get caught in between the vise grip of gloating over past glories or fearing the struggles of the future. Both mindsets have a similar effect. They keep the man and/or team out of the present and stuck in the quicksand of "maybes" and "what-ifs". Paralyzed, those caught in this trap have lost the season even before the first snap.

"Believe in Now." How interesting that the league would "preach" what the church has been promoting for centuries. In fact, it was the church's "head coach," Jesus, who first promoted this concept. Take a look in our "playbook" (Bible). Jesus admonished the gathered crowd to "not worry about tomorrow" (Matthew 6:34).

Apparently, that generation struggled with the worries of the future just as we do today. But it wasn't just provisions for and success in the future that those first-century Christians worried about. Paul had to "coach up" the newly born church against worrying about the past. He exhorted them to follow his lead in "forgetting what is behind" (Philippians 3:13).

If Jesus was telling us to believe in now, what would He be telling us? I think He would be coaching us:

- to seek His kingdom and His purposes (Matthew 6:33),
- and to press on toward our heavenly prize (Philippians 3:14).

"Believe in Now." The league got this one right.

## Study the Playbook

**READ:** Matthew 6:19–21, 25–33

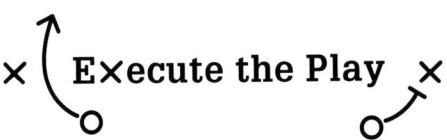

Do you find yourself wrestling with anxiety? Write down all of your fears. Now read them as a prayer. Slip this list into an envelope and keep it hidden in your Bible. Let God surprise you with how He will answer your most secret needs.

# Can I Have Your Autograph?

**T**raining camp, the end of a game, half-time by the tunnel, on the sidelines, special appearances and signings—what do they all have in common? Fans hanging around asking players for their autographs.

From the point of view of the avid fan or the aspiring athlete, to be a star player in the NFL is to have arrived. Now fast-forward twenty years. No more football. The season of life that included the NFL is a sweet but swiftly fading memory. No more fans clamoring for autographs. It's ironic. How can a person be so prominent for one generation and yet a relatively unknown figure for the next?

It would seem that the human population is very fickle or, at the least, quite forgetful. But that is the nature of man. Thankfully, that is not God's way. Moses tells us the way God relates to us.

"He will be with you; He will not leave you nor forsake you; do not fear nor be dismayed" (Deuteronomy 31:8, NKJV).

Yes, perhaps like you, I will go on collecting autographs to display in my game room. Yet my most cherished one is the one written on the tablet of my heart. It reads:

I have loved you with an everlasting love ... (Jeremiah 31:3, NKJV).

Abba/God

## Study the Playbook

READ: 1 Peter 5:7; John 3:16;
Ephesians 2:4–5; Psalm 36:7

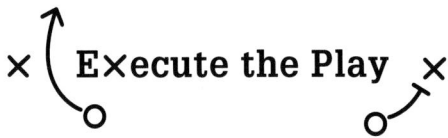

## Execute the Play

Keep one (or more) of these Scriptures posted by your mirror. Every day, read at least one of these verses to the person you see looking back at you in the mirror. See what kind of autograph God will write on your heart.

_____

_____

_____

_____

_____

# December

At the beginning of the season, along with the rest of you NFL faithful, I made my predictions for which teams would make it to the Super Bowl. December rolls along, and with that comes winter and the gaze toward the playoffs. Although both teams I had tagged were still in contention, other teams I thought wouldn't even make an appearance were closing in on playoff berths. Strange how life brings the unexpected, isn't it?

Six teams had already been eliminated from the race. There wasn't a chance for them to make it, even as a wild card. I watched their training camps. Using the highest quality equipment that money can buy, talented athletes were put through demanding, disciplined workouts under the guidance of veteran and previous Super Bowl champion coaches. Everyone involved was baffled as to what happened and what went wrong. But if we look closer, we can find a surprising number of strange and unexpected injuries. Regardless of preparation and protection, sometimes injuries take out some of the best athletes. Unfortunately, it is one of the sad facts of football. Injury is the silent enemy of all athletes. While some teams have enough talent and depth that they can recover from the loss of a key player, there is almost no team that can withstand the loss of multiple key players from the roster.

December is also a time when the rest of the world begins to take inventory of the year. When you rang in the New Year, did you ever dream of the events which have transpired? While at lunch with some friends, we began to look at the year in review. Mirroring some of the NFL teams, they too had had a Cinderella year with engagements, graduations, or the birth of a child. But my year had resembled more the teams out of contention, one full of losses. With a job loss and the death of a dear loved one, the year had left me wondering what went wrong. Like the teams plagued with injuries, sometimes losses come—not so much because of wrongs committed, but just from living life in a fragile and fallen world. How easy it is for disillusionment and discouragement to set in.

Yet, in the midst of a season of sorrows, God offers us words of comfort. Jesus quoted His Father's promise as recorded by the prophet Isaiah: "A bruised reed He will not break" (Matthew 12:20).

You and I might feel as if we are at a breaking point, but our loving Father assures us that His grace is sufficient for us and that His strength is made perfect in our weaknesses (2 Corinthians 12:9). Remember, win or lose, He is faithful to see us through another December.

# Study the Playbook

**READ:** 2 Corinthians 12:9–10;
Romans 5:5; Psalm 46:1, 147:11

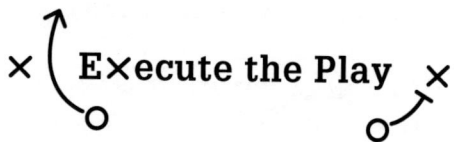

## Execute the Play

Stop the replay of what all has gone wrong. Start keeping a list of how God is bringing you through life's hurdles and into victory with Him.

# Eating Humble Pie

I've never spent a day as a rookie on any NFL team, but I've heard some pretty interesting stories of the challenges they have to face. One particular tradition has caught my attention: the rookie rite of passage. They have to serve both veteran players and coaches alike. Mundane chores and tasks are given to the rookies. To an outsider, these actions might seem harsh and unnecessary. Most certainly, the rookie would concur. Yet, ask that same rookie his opinion again, once he's a veteran player of several years, and you're likely to hear a totally different appraisal.

You see, when coaches and veteran players are serving humble pie to the rookies, their general intent is to strengthen the character of the young players. Their goal is to build, not break the rookie. What coaches know is how awfully hard it is to teach something new to a superstar. *Why,* he thinks he's arrived and needs nothing but others to bow down and adore him! Not all rookies come into camp full of themselves. But it is wisdom that directs us to require much to whom much has been given. When an athlete is given multi-million dollar contracts, with hefty bonuses as well, it is more than fair to hold them to equally high standards of excellence, both on and off the field. During the process, a rookie might not think he's being given a fair shot and that many of his teammates have it out for him. Yet, in due time, if he perseveres he will emerge a better, more mature player.

Can you identify with this rookie? If you're feeling like life is handing you some humble pie, be assured you're not alone. The early Christians experienced similar heart challenges. James admonished them (and us) to, "Humble yourselves before the Lord, and He will exalt you" (James 4:10, NRS).

Having a teachable attitude is the milk that helps to wash down that tart humble pie. Bon appétit!

## Study the Playbook

**READ:** John 15:16; 2 Peter 3:18; Colossians 1:28

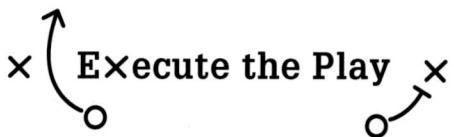

## Execute the Play

You've been given someone who is leading and coaching you to become the best that you can be. Today, commit to listen, learn and apply all that you're being taught. It won't be long before you grow to be a champion.

# Fair-weather Fan

We've heard football fans described as dedicated, devoted, committed, fanatical, frenzied, and even crazy. But no fan ever wants to be tagged with the label of fair-weather fan. What does that label mean? That label would be a painful insult, because it would mean this person is:

- all for the home team when they're winning. But when they're losing, he packs up early and leaves the stadium so he can beat the traffic out of the parking lot.

- the one who has all the authentic apparel the NFL has licensed for *the* team. But it's this same person who wouldn't be caught dead in the team jersey after they've lost a game.

- the fan who paints his face in team colors and yells the loudest for the team. Yet, it's the same person who joins right in with the rest of the crew that's bad-mouthing the team for such a "sorry" season.

- is all smiles as the team's number-one fan when things are going well. But when the scoreboard starts to show losses, this fan has disappeared like a mist on a hot summer morning.

Sad to say, too many people handle their personal relationships the same way. They are fair-weather friends. Sure, they're there when life is treating you well, when there's plenty of money in your bank account and you keep your problems to yourself. But let a hint of trouble slip into the conversation and they are nowhere to be found.

Even more tragic is that too many in the church behave in the same manner. But it shouldn't be so. According to the wisest man in history, Solomon counseled that a good friend is so reliable that he's closer than a brother (Proverbs 18:24b). And Jesus not only told but also modeled for us that a true friend is willing to lay his life down for another (John 15:13). Just what does that type of friend look like today? Maybe it's setting the game to record when a friend is going through some tough times and needs some-one to talk to. Or perhaps it's pitching in to help your buddy move when you'd rather sit out the afternoon with ESPN and a tall glass of lemonade. It's helping to shoulder the "heavy" times of life, when our flesh cries out, "Let someone else do it!" Since Jesus was the ultimate model of a true friend, that means we're called to share a bit of "Son-shine" in our friend's dark hour. Come on, grab your "Son-glasses" and let's go.

"There is a friend who sticks closer than a brother" (Proverbs 18:24b).

# Study the Playbook

**READ:** Ecclesiastes 4:9–12; John 15:12–13; Proverb 17:17; Romans 12:15; Proverbs 18:24

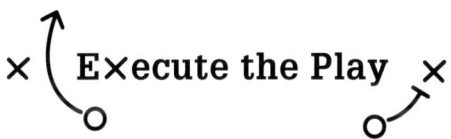

## Execute the Play

The next time your friend calls with a need, if you are able to meet that need, don't put it off or make excuses why you can't. Don't stay on the sidelines. Get in the game and provide some real defense for your friend.

_____

_____

_____

_____

_____

_____

_____

_____

_____

_____

# Going to the Market

Have you ever watched one of those national beauty pageants? As all the lovely young ladies parade before us and the judges, it's as if they're asking "Mirror, Mirror, on the wall, who's the fairest of them all?" Each young woman is trying to sell the judges that she is indeed the most beautiful and talented of them all. Can't help but think it's a charade at best; at worst, it's a meat market.

Okay. Before you peg me as sexist (or what ever label is floating in your mind), let me share that I think there is another such market. But this one is on the "super market" scale. Yes, I'm pointing a finger at the Scouting Combine. In late February of each year, teams send out their scouts to hunt for that star athlete who just might take them to the Super Bowl. They come with their shopping list. The fastest. The strongest. The highest jumper. The best hands. Of course, it's important to have a fair system of assessing talent. I'm not knocking the validity of knowledge, especially as it applies to making wise investments. But here is my concern: GMs, owners, and coaches line up to watch the parade of the finest and newest on the market. It sounds like I'm talking about an exotic car. And that's the problem. When did the game turn into a business that looks at a man as no more than a valuable piece of property?

Each man who takes the field is someone's son, brother, father, husband, friend. He is so much more than another prized acquisition. How is it that a mere mortal thinks he can own another? Yet, each generation has fallen prey to this faulty notion. Think about:

- the greed driven slave trader and the self indulgent rich with their "stock" of slaves
- the "popular" teens and "their" followers
- the pimp and his street corner prostitutes.
- the boss and "his" employees
- the owners and "their" players

It's a sobering thought. Whether physical, emotional or spiritual, it seems that too many are still held as captives. Feeling empty and alone, life's struggles can pose the question if a life has any purpose or value. Does the Bible have anything to say about this dilemma? Thankfully, yes. God reminds us that He created us, and masterfully so. Furthermore, Jesus taught us that we are priceless. We are so valuable to Him that He bought us with His own life (1 Corinthians 6:20). And unlike the stock market (or a football team), He will never sell or trade us. Now that truth is a priceless investment we can buy into.

"For you created my inmost being; you knit me together in my mother's womb. I praise you because I am fearfully and wonderfully made; your works are wonderful, I know that full well" (Psalm 139:13–14).

## Study the Playbook

**READ:** Genesis 1:27; 1 John 4:10; Acts 17:28a; John 8:32; Psalm 118:8; Proverbs 3:26

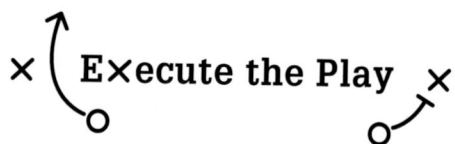

## Execute the Play

Look up and print out these (and other affirming) verses. Post them by the mirror, or in the car…somewhere you can see them daily. Read them aloud each day. Practice them in your mind until you own the truth that you are valuable to God!

_____

_____

_____

_____

_____

_____

# He Just Walked Away

On January 12, 2009, Tony Dungy announced his retirement. After three decades in the league; 148 wins; an unmatched ten consecutive play-off seasons; six consecutive twelve-win seasons, the league's highest average of regular season victories of *any* coach; and the rare status as a Super Bowl winning coach, he just walked away. It seems unimaginable that a man, still young at fifty-three, would walk away from all the glory, fame, and a salary exceeding $5 million!

If we went looking for Tony, we might expect that he would be golfing at the most elite country clubs, sailing on a yacht or jetting off to some fabulous resort for some much earned R & R. Perhaps you would think to find him at another book signing, having authored three books already. NBC did manage to bring him on board for the Sunday Night games as a color analyst. While it's a quality experience, it certainly is not a full time vocation. If Tony wanted another career, the speaking engagements offered to him would be more than enough to fill a calendar year. President Obama wanted him as council member for a faith-based, neighborhood partnership. DeMaurice Smith, the executive director of the NFL Players Association, wanted him to serve as a liaison. Yet, Tony has respectfully declined these appealing offers.

So just where would one go to find Tony when he's not spending quality time with his family? You can probably find Tony Dungy in prison. But not as an inmate. He's often a special guest at one of the prisons in Florida or Indiana. Not afraid to get in the midst of those he's reaching out to, he brings the message of hope and redemption to men incarcerated for some pretty hefty crimes. Why would Coach Dungy just walk away from all that he had in the NFL to preach the gospel of Christ to a group of inmates? To understand that way of thinking, we have to look at God's sense of economy. Jesus told us and His disciples,

> Do not store up for yourselves treasures on earth, where moth and rust destroy and where thieves break in and steal. But store up for yourselves treasures in heaven, where moth and rust do not destroy and thieves do not break in and steal. For where your treasure is, there your heart will be also.
>
> Matthew 6:19–21

Our society doesn't understand why so many brilliant individuals turn away from six figure incomes to opt for less paying careers. Teachers, nurses and paramedics, ministers, police officers, fire fighters and stay at home moms: it is this group of people who have molded and influenced our lives most. To the world, it might not make any sense why Tony just walked away from a lucrative and prestigious career in the NFL. But that's okay. Coach Dungy didn't just walk away; he walked into a new direction of vocational ministry. Sounds like he's on his way to another winning season.

## Study the Playbook

**READ:** Proverbs 27:9; Acts 13:15; Galatians 6:7–10; 1 Thessalonians 5:12

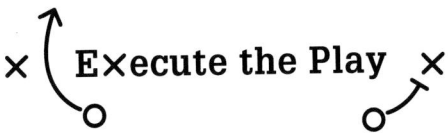

As your path crosses with those in public service, be sure to offer genuine praise and thanks for their hard work. Take it up one notch and compliment them and their efforts to their employer.

# I Love Me Some Me

I f you've been catching any behind-the-scenes footage of the NFL, you've most likely heard Terrell Owens adamantly say, "I love me some me." When I first heard him say that, I thought, *How incredibly arrogant.* Did his comment aggravate you too? Thankfully, it got under my skin so much that it made me think. I had to dissect the comment to see if it really was an arrogant statement or not.

When I come across something that doesn't seem quite right, I am reminded that God directs us to check out the content of every message.

"Test everything. Hold on to the good" (1 Thessalonians 5:21).

"Do not believe every spirit, but test the spirits to see whether they are from God" (1 John 4:1).

While I thought Terrell's statement was arrogant, it turned out that he was scripturally correct and relevant. I know. It shocked me too. Take a look at Matthew 22:39. Jesus actually *commanded*, "Love your neighbor as yourself." Now, I've seen how some people love themselves. It resembles more loathing that loving. Of course, we know that self-loathing is birthed out of condemnation. But that's another topic for another day. Back to the subject at hand. How should we love self? Are we to love ourselves in a narcissistic, worldly way? Absolutely not. We are to follow God's design. He laid out the blueprint that shows how we are to believe His truths over the devil's lies. God tells us that we were:

- created by Him (Psalm 139:14)
- created for His purposes (Ephesians 2:10)
- created in His image (Genesis 1:27)
- redeemed by Christ (1 Corinthians 6:20)
- adopted as joint heirs with Jesus (Romans 8:17)
- loved with His everlasting love (Jeremiah 31:3)

As it turns out, it is *not* arrogant to love oneself but rather a demonstration and application of trust in God and His Word. Hopefully, this brief investigation has encouraged you to dare to look at the person in your mirror and say, "I love me some me."

## Study the Playbook

**READ:** the Scripture verses listed above.

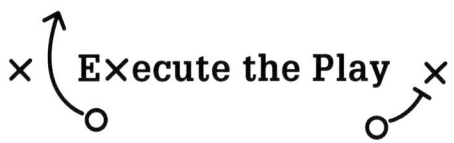

### Execute the Play

Print out these verses and carry them with you every day. Read them aloud each day. Do this until they are locked solidly in your memory.

# Job Security?

I n an era of recession, the concern about job security can create an atmosphere of anxiety. Every year, during the off-season, several key players are released from their teams. Oftentimes, these are well-established, high-impact players. Speculations abound as to why they were released:

- the team is changing its offense or defense;
- the player is not the right size, weight, or speed for the new strategy;
- the player asked for a sweeter contract.

Whatever the reason(s), one thing is clear. Those players won't be wearing the same jersey come game day.

Promises, agreements, and contracts all look and sound great at the time; but the bottom line is that nothing in this world is permanent. There is no such thing as job security in the NFL. Security in this world is as elusive a dream as cotton candy is at lasting in the mouth. In a time when the need for security is at a global high, it appears it is the least available.

Where we need stability, it seems that too much of life is in a constant state of transition.

Is there any hope for security? Yes. God tells us He is the same, yesterday, today, and tomorrow (Hebrews 13:8). In Deuteronomy 31:8, our Father tells us that He will never leave nor forsake us. The Scriptures are very clear in declaring that God is our Provider (Philippians 4:19). Finally, Jesus instructs us to place our focus on Him and His kingdom purposes and He will continue to provide for our needs (Matthew 6:33).

Job security is a myth in this world, but *true security* is completely real in God for all eternity!

"And my God will meet all your needs according to his glorious riches in Christ Jesus" (Philippians 4:19).

# Study the Playbook

**READ:** Matthew 6:25–33; Luke 12:22–31

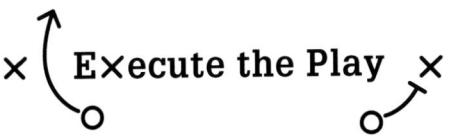

## Execute the Play

Every time you find yourself beginning to worry, stop. Read these verses. Think of five things for which you are thankful. Write them down. Now tell God thank you for these blessings He has given to you. Watch that spirit of anxiety shrink away!

# Cirque du Sidelines

The players on the bench. The host of coaches. The trainers, team doctors. The water boy. The event/security staff in neon yellow shirts. Cheerleaders in the four corners. Music blasting from the sound system. The team mascot riding around in the end zone on his motorcycle. The privileged few with a sideline pass. The media hovering around with their cameras. It's amazing how anyone can stay focused on the game with so many diversions! Why, we could say it was like a sideline circus.

Maybe you feel like you're in the midst of a sideline circus. Appointments. Meetings. Rush-hour traffic. Soccer games. Pee Wee football practice. Piano lessons. Church choir rehearsal. Grocery shopping. Cutting the lawn. Homework with the kids. Dinner with the in-laws. Balance the checkbook. Pay the bills. With the nonstop whirl of our hectic lives, how can anyone stay focused on God and His plans for our life?

Paul faced a similar challenge. He was a Roman citizen and a Messianic Jew. He had three different groups of people all clamoring for his time, loyalty, and energies. Talk about trying to balance a multi-faceted life. His life could have resembled a circus, but he chose to stay focused on Christ. Paul put it this way: "One thing I do: forgetting what is behind and reaching forward to what is ahead, I pursue as my goal the prize promised by God's heavenly call in Christ Jesus" (Philippians 3:13–14, HCSB).

We can focus on Christ. And as we do, He will bring order and direction to our lives. We need to put on spiritual blinders and keep our eyes trained on our Lord Jesus. He will surely help us cross over the goal line into His victory.

## Study the Playbook

READ: Isaiah 26:3; Matthew 11:28;
Luke 10:38–42; Philippians 4:13

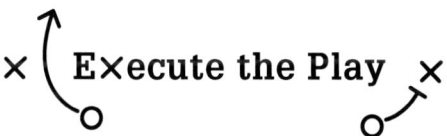

## Execute the Play

When you're starting to feel overwhelmed by responsibilities, stop the whirlwind. Sit down. Return to the basics. Remember what tasks God has given to you. Focus on Him. Now, look at the most pressing task. Tackle it first. Now you're on track!

# Leaving on a Jet Plane

**H**ave you looked at the new fall schedule? What teams are we playing away? For the fan, it might not mean too many changes logistically. The fan might choose home, a friend's place, or a local sports restaurant to enjoy the game. But for the players, it can become a major challenge. The flight takes them away from home and family to a lonely hotel room filled with the challenge of numerous temptations. Rivers of alcoholic drinks flow almost as fast as the "free" women who throw themselves at the men for an evening of "fun". Poker games, gambling and illicit drugs are readily available for the right price. And porn is only a click away. Lowered accountability and greater opportunity often end in losses of another kind: losses of the heart.

We've read the newspapers and heard the reports. Too often, there is yet another scandal that adds one more blemish to the face of football. Paul discussed the issue of temptation with Timothy. He said, "Those who desire to be rich fall into temptation and a snare, and into many foolish and harmful lusts which drown men in destruction and perdition" (1 Timothy 6:9, NKJV).

It's pretty easy to sit on the sidelines and penalize the players for their losses to temptation. "Why, they're paid millions of dollars for each season. They must all be spoiled, undisciplined, and a menace to society." These are some of the judgments handed down from the fans. But this is where we must be careful. Jesus said that in the same manner we judge others, we will be judged (Matthew 7:1–2). If the camera was turned onto our lives, would the reporters turn up any hidden dirt ?

- Can't stay away from the refrigerator?

- Spent the rent money at the local bar?

- Caught in a web of Internet pornography?

- Gossiping about co-workers?

- Blew the light bill money on the weekend trip to the casino?

- Just can't give up those cigarettes?

- The grocery money bought your "high" from the drug dealer?

Having reviewed a list of those clandestine vices, I guess it's not too attractive to have a judgmental attitude, is it? We all have our own struggles. As for you, me, and all those high-paid players, God's mercy and provision are the same. He promises us a way to escape from that seemingly unbearable temptation

(1 Corinthians 10:13). But it's up to us. We must choose to flee temptation. Our reward will be the trophy of trust from those we love.

## Study the Playbook

**READ:** Ecclesiastes 4:9–12;
Philippians 4:13; 2 Corinthians 10:5b

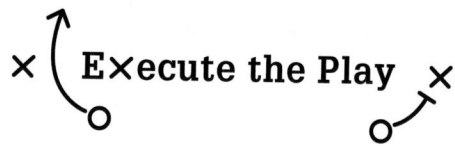

Know the areas of temptation you tend to fall prey to. Plan ahead. Prepare yourself so that you don't have to face them alone. NEVER put yourself in a situation where you are alone with the object of your temptation. Memorize these and other battle readying verses. Say them aloud when you feel temptation is trying to tackle you. Get out of the situation before you become tomorrow's news!

# Made and Broken but Hard to Keep

**S**ounds like clues in a riddle, but this is no joke. I'm talking about promises. How many promises did the franchise make to you? They were easy to make and just as easy to break. Too many times, they promised you would start. But that was little consolation while you sat and watched a teammate take the field in your stead. Years and injuries later, you wait to see if the league will honor its promise to take care of your health needs. When you were young and at peak strength, they promised to be there for you no matter what injury came. But now that you're not packing their stadiums, it's not so easy for them to stand by that early promise.

We see these same types of patterns in all walks of life. Just think back on your high school days. You and your best buds promised to be together for all time. Do you even know where they are now? When young couples are goofy and giddy, it's easy to promise forever love. Trials and hardships later, too many find it easier to break their promises than to weather the storms. Businesses and companies promise benefits, stocks, and a potential of great wealth. But when life puts a squeeze on their profits and lifestyles, watch how easy it is for them to declare bankruptcy and rid themselves of promises, employees, and responsibilities.

Standing in the wake of too many broken promises can make a person jaded. You find yourself leery of trusting again. Worse yet, you find it difficult (or almost impossible) to trust God. Apparently, He understood that we would need reassurance. Like our business contracts or wedding rings, God gave us symbols to remind us of His promises. Here's an example. After the great flood, God promised all of humanity that He would never destroy the world again by water. He marked that promise with the rainbow (Genesis 9:12–17). Better yet, our Master promised that He would adopt us as His own. He marked that promise with the cross (Ephesians 1:5). He sealed that promise for all time with His Holy Spirit (Romans 8:14–17, 2 Corinthians 1:22).

Since we see that God is faithful to keep His promises, it's only fair that He expects something in return from you and me. Jesus said, "Simply let your 'yes' be 'yes' and your 'no', 'no'" (Matthew 5:37). He expects and requires us to follow His example. Whether others are faithful to us and their word, as heirs and ambassadors of God, we are to keep the promises we make. Then our lives will be living proofs of our God's character as the great Promise-Keeper.

# Study the Playbook

**READ:** Matthew 19:6; Matthew 5:33–37;
Numbers 30:2; Ecclesiastes 5:4–7

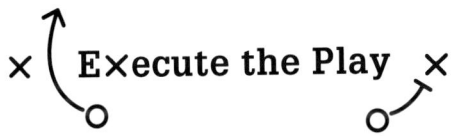

## Execute the Play

Every day, in all your dealings, be full of integrity, always keeping your word. Ask a close friend to hold you accountable to keeping all that you've promised.

# Not Today

The running back has his goal in sight. All week he has trained to run to the end zone. It has been his motivation. It is his purpose. But there are those who would stop him from reaching victory. From the corner of his eye, the back sees his opponent angling in. He "stiff-arms" his would-be tackler. Welling up from deep within is his warrior spirit that cries out, "Not today!" Locked out, the defensive player slips down while the back races on to score.

Could this scene describe your life? With your goal in sight, does it feel like your opponent is angling in against you? You know he wants nothing more than to bring you down. Bills are mounting. Income is short. Fatigue is setting in. Responsibilities keep coming. You hear your would-be captor whispering doubts in your mind. "Think you can make it? Are you sure? Why not quit and stop the pain of an inevitable loss?"

King David faced a similar battle. His foes were camped around him. They taunted him, "Where is your God?" David was discouraged. Doubts of potential defeat were poised to drown him.

"Why are you downcast, O my soul? Why so disturbed within me?" (Psalm 42:5).

But then it was as if his warrior spirit rose up within him. He opposed his enemy with truth. He reclaimed God's direction in his life by declaring, "Put your hope in God, for I will yet praise him, my Savior and my God" (Psalm 42:5).

When your enemy comes against you with doubts and discouragement, "stiff-arm" him and shout, "Not today!"

## Study the Playbook

READ: Philippians 4:6–8, 13; Deuteronomy 31:6; John 14:1

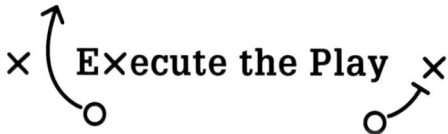

### Execute the Play

Learn these (and other) "can-do" Bible verses. Say them out loud whenever you feel discouragement closing in on you.

_____

_____

_____

_____

_____

# Obsolete

The Super Bowl is over. For the next few months the team will savor the sweet taste of victory and the elusive title of world champions. They finally reached the pinnacle of the National Football League. What's more, they emerged victorious. How long will they get to enjoy their title? Well past the trip to Disney World, and maybe far into the season. But it's only a rare few who make a return trip to the Super Bowl, much less bring home the Lombardi again. Most likely, this year's Super Bowl champion will become obsolete sometime within the next twelve months.

Super Bowl champions aren't the only ones to become obsolete. Take a trip to your local electronics store and you'll see that your "steal of a deal" purchase was because it has been discontinued. It has become obsolete. A newer, better version/model has been released. We see this pattern repeating itself in the fashion and automotive worlds, too. What was the hottest item last year is now viewed with distaste and disdain, or simply forgotten.

Check the classifieds. Employers are clamoring for younger, more technologically savvy employees.

For the growing masses of those poor souls holding a pink slip, they know they've been replaced by a newer model. In essence, they've become obsolete.

Take a look at our divorce courts. Individuals who were once happily married couples purposely stand in line to dispose of a relationship that was to last for all time. They too are declaring their marriage to be obsolete.

In a world that longs for stability and something constant, is there anything or anyone who can withstand the winds of change? Thankfully, there is. Let me introduce you to my friend, Jesus. He is, "the same yesterday and today and forever" (Hebrews 13:8).

Everything in our world is subject to becoming obsolete, but Jesus is eternal. He will never expire or be replaced. He is the one and only Savior, the One we can count on past the end of time.

## Study the Playbook

**READ:** Psalm 100:1–5; Revelation 1:8; Isaiah 57:15

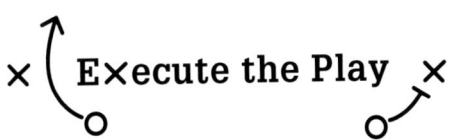

## Execute the Play

If you find yourself beginning to slide down into despair, create a checklist of all the times God has come through for you. Remember five times God has stood by you when others were not present. Thank Him for being steadfast and faithful.

# Playing for an Audience of One

Camera crews, ball boys, teammates, the visiting team, as well as the dance team were all in full swing of the pregame activities. Honestly, it was quite a hub of action. Yet, in the very center was a lone man. Finished with his pre-game warm-up and stretches, he made his way to the team logo and knelt. For a moment, it was as if time stood still. The noise from the PA system continued to blast out announcements. Athletes and support personnel kept on with their list of important tasks. The stands began to fill with fans. In the midst of noise and anticipation, this one man remained, undaunted and unaffected. For him, the stands were empty, save One.

Seems odd, doesn't it? A brief kneel, a quick point heavenward, or an unobtrusive signing of the cross have become fairly common. As such, they have gained a certain level of tolerance from the world. But this... this was different. He never looked up. He never made a sound. He just knelt and kept on kneeling. What a powerful message this one proclaimed with his simple act of devoted worship. And what was the message? It was the same as Paul's declaration, "I am not ashamed of the Gospel, because it is the power of God for the salvation of everyone who believes" (Romans 1:16).

This week, around the office water cooler, in the faculty lounge or locker room, how will we respond? Given the opportunity, I pray that you and I will remember that we too are "playing for an audience of One."

> "Whoever acknowledges me before men, I will also acknowledge him before My Father in heaven" (Matthew 10:32).

## Study the Playbook

**READ:** John 1:40–42; Matthew 4:18–22

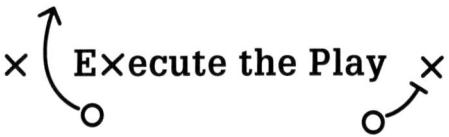

# Execute the Play

Begin developing a personal plan of introducing everyone you know and meet to your best friend, Jesus. This week, invite a friend to chapel services, Bible study, or church. Whenever you go out for a meal, leave a witnessing tract with your (generous) tip.

# Ready and Able

**D**uring an interview, Andy Talley, Villanova's head coach, was asked about number 20, Brian Westbrook. Coach Talley noted that Brian is a rare talent. Not many running backs are good at running, catching, and playing on special teams. It was apparent that Brian was not only able but that he was always ready. When Coach Talley met with Eagles head coach, Andy Reid, before the 2002 draft, he recommended his number 20. As they say, the rest is history.

It's not enough for a player to like football. The coach has to know that his player is ready and able. *Ready* speaks to preparation and an attitude of willingness. An athlete is ready when he is suited up in full uniform, has studied and is competent with the plays, has given his all in practice, and is pumped for action. *Able* tells what the athlete actually can do based on his physical design and state of health. Having the ability and paying the price of readiness, the player will soon be recognized as a true pro.

These truths apply to everyday life as well. It's not enough to show up to work. We must be ready: study the notes, prepare the documents, and be dressed for success. All tools and props must be secured and implemented. We must also be able: in good health, with sufficient rest, and competent to carry out whatever task is given.

Our Christian life is much the same. It's not enough to sit back, complacently waiting for the return of Christ. As players on God's team, we must show our coach, Jesus, that we are ready and able to play out the game of godly living. Follow Paul's instructions: "Concentrate on doing your best for God, work you won't be ashamed of, laying out the truth plain and simple" (2 Timothy 2:15, MSG).

*Ready:* get baptized. Read and study the Bible. Pray for sinners, yourself, and other saints. Attend and serve in the local church. Share the good news with everyone God leads you to. *Able*: receive Christ as your personal Savior. That makes you God's adopted heir. Now you're ready and able.

## Study the Playbook

READ: Romans 12:3–5; 1 Corinthians 10:31–33; Colossians 3:14–16; Ephesians 2:19–22

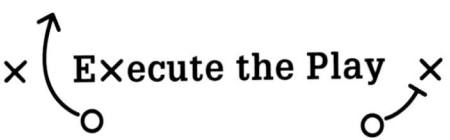

### Execute the Play

Don't be just a spectator or critic. Get involved in your local church. Take a spiritual gifts class to see where you would be best qualified to serve. Volunteer and be faithful to follow through with what you commit to do.

# Second Chances

As I sit here looking at my adorable puppy Levi, I wonder if I would have been as merciful and forgiving. Of course, I'm talking about Michael Vick. Come on now, all of you dog lovers out there. If we're being honest, we've all struggled with feelings of judgment when we heard the news of what he had done. And we've doubted the genuineness of the change of heart and mind that he's professed. There are those reading this who think Michael got off way too easy. Fortunately for Vick, Commissioner Goodell has been more merciful. He has given Michael a second chance at this once-in-a-lifetime opportunity.

UNDER HIS HELMET

Just when you and I are thinking that we're so righteous, we should review our past. I know I haven't been perfect. What about you? Do your yesterdays hold sins you'd rather have forgotten? We all have moments that we would like to have erased from our past. It all boils down to this: it's a good thing that grace and mercy are not given based on our worthiness. God forgives and redeems us because it pleases Him to do so. We don't deserve it, but He gives these gifts to us because He is a loving and merciful Father. In fact, the Psalmist describes God's relationship to us this way:

> He does not treat us as our sins deserve or repay us according to our iniquities. For as high as the heavens are above the earth, so great is His love for those who fear Him; as far as the east is from the west, so far has He removed our transgressions from us.
>
> Psalm 103:10–12

If you or I were sitting on God's throne, life would have a very different outcome. The judgment and condemnation we dish out to ourselves and others would not leave many people standing. But thank the Lord that He is God and we are not. His mercy and grace are His gifts to us. Don't just stand there. Go open your gifts!

## Study the Playbook

**READ:** Matthew 7:1–5; Romans 2:1–3; James 4:11–12

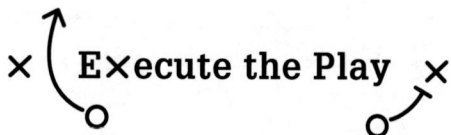

## Execute the Play

The next time you start to judge someone else, pull out a sheet of paper. Fold it in half. On the left side, write down all the wrongs done by this one who has offended you. On the right side, write down every wrong and sin you've committed. Think of the grace you are wanting. Is it deserved? Pray for mercy and forgiveness … for both you and your offender.

# Target Locked

Target locked: it's a military term used by fighter pilots. It means the target has been acquired, is in the sights, and is locked for destruction. These words create an image that is powerful and chilling.

This reminds me of a certain Hall-of-Famer. He was known for his piercing stare, one that could intimidate any opponent. Once his sight locked on his target, that play was over. Mr. Intensity. Leading headfirst and cracking sixteen helmets during his tenure as a Baylor Bear, it's easy to see how he might earn the moniker of Samurai Mike. This man has staggering statistics: named to the All-Southwest Conference Team of the 1970s and 1980s; second-round draft pick; twelve years in the league; ten straight Pro Bowls (eight All-Pro); 172 pro starts; 1,488 tackles (885 solo); nineteen sacks; seven interceptions; and the proud owner of a Super Bowl XX ring. So great was his level of play that he was voted one of the top one hundred players of all time. Meet linebacker "par excellence" Mike Singletary.

Whether as a Baylor or Chicago Bear, Mike only knew one speed: full throttle. As a father of seven children and husband to Kim, his only wife of twenty-five plus years, he has the passion to be a servant leader. As a head coach in the NFL (San Francisco Forty-niners), he has the drive to train each man to be his best. As a motivational speaker and an author of multiple books , he yearns to draw others to greatness. Yet most of all, his heart's greatest desire is to be a champion for Christ. In his daily walk, Mike lives out what Paul taught the Colossian Christians: "Whatever you do, work at it with all your heart, as working for the Lord, not for men" (Colossians 3:23).

Like Mike, set your sights on excellence and lock on your target of obedience. May we all carry his same intensity for serving and pleasing our Lord.

## Study the Playbook

**READ:** 1 Peter 1:7, 4:11;
1 Chronicles 16:8–9; Jeremiah 9:24

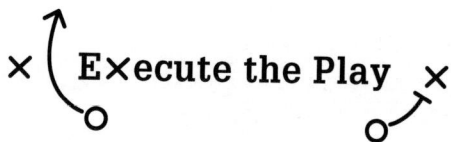

## Execute the Play

Whatever you do, do it to a standard of excellence. And when someone compliments you on a job well done, thank them and take advantage of this opportunity to direct the praise and glory to God.

# The Color of Football

From its inception and during its infancy, it used to be white. Now, it's black, brown, red, yellow, and white. No, the pigskin hasn't changed its color. But the faces of the men who play the game now have a very different look. A once racially segregated game has come to reflect America's melting pot. If the Statue of Liberty can bid a kind welcome to people of all colors, why has it been so difficult for the game to follow suit?

During the early years, men of color (any other than white) were forbidden to play the game. What drove so many to such a rabid position against others of a different race? Whatever the toxin, it was sufficient to poison entire generations.

Then time ushered in the '60s. Players of color began to enter the picture. Distrust and tension reached an excruciating high. Coach Boone of T.C. Williams High School (Alexandria, Virginia) was all too familiar with the conflict brought about through

racial discrimination and hatred. Those of us who love
the game of football will always remember the Titans.
Coach Boone fought a formidable opponent: racism.
The battle waged on, but he eventually emerged victorious. Those who had once declared a bitter distaste
for the other pledged their allegiance to one another.
Foes had become friends.

Almost fifty years later, and the war against racism still has not been won. We still see distrust and
tension between players. Racism is not quarantined to
football though. We see its effects around the water
cooler, the children's soccer games, the local restaurant, and our neighborhood markets. Worse yet, racism has slithered its way into God's house. Already
fragmented by denominations, the church has allowed
our supernatural foe to further divide us with this
insidious toxin. The body of Christ has been segregated. Many even believe that heaven itself will be
segregated. We must ask the question: *at Calvary, did
Christ's blood flow just for a few?* God forbid. As Pastor Dwight McKissic says, "The church should mirror
the multitudes of heaven."* Red, yellow, black, brown,
and white, we are all precious in His sight.

> If you really keep the royal law found in Scripture,
> "Love your neighbor as yourself," you are doing
> right. But if you show favoritism, you sin and are
> convicted by the law as lawbreakers. For whoever
> keeps the whole law and yet stumbles at just one
> point is guilty of breaking all of it.
>
> James 2:8–10

# Study the Playbook

**READ:** Galatians 3:28; Acts 10:34; James 2:4

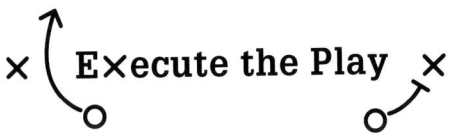

## Execute the Play

It may be time to get your vision checked. When you see a person, look PAST the color of his skin. See the person. See the relationship you are developing or have. Focus on the valuable qualities this person has to offer.

*Reverend Wm. Dwight McKissic is the senior pastor of Cornerstone Baptist Church in Arlington, Texas.

_____

_____

_____

_____

_____

_____

_____

_____

# Heart on a String

Who knew? In 1991, the Falcons had their second-round draft pick sitting out as their second-string quarterback. He just didn't fit into their plans. He warmed the bench for all the season games, save two. It would have been easy for this man to become discouraged and settle for what looked like his destiny. He could have easily resigned his heart to disillusionment, bitterness, and mediocrity. Yet, he persevered. He continued to work hard. Two decades later, anywhere you see that number 4 on his jersey you see a symbol of athletic excellence. That jersey belongs to Brett Favre. He didn't give up. He kept on keeping on. And he has emerged a gridiron champion.

Think about that prize or goal you yearn to attain. Your dream may seem impossibly out of reach. It could be that job promotion; a first-string position; or a healthy, loving marriage. Or perhaps it's a creative venture that is new and exciting but also feels threatening. Sometimes the circumstances in life seem overwhelming. The soul can become weary. It would be so easy, so comfortable to give in to the softness of

incompletion. But could you face that pain when you look into those eyes staring back at you in the mirror? No? Then take heart. You are not the first to struggle. Paul had to encourage the weary in Galatia. He implored them (and us all) to "not grow weary while doing good, for in due season we shall reap if we do not lose heart" (Galatians 6:9, NKJV).

Set your eyes on excellence and your feet into action. Victory might be just a heartbeat away.

## Study the Playbook

**READ:** Isaiah 40:28–31;
Romans 8:28–29; Genesis 32:24–26

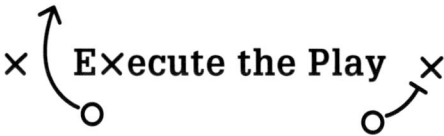

Write out your God-given dream. Create a plan, based on achievable goals. Break it down into daily steps to implement. Ask a trusted friend to encourage and hold you accountable. Don't let fear make you wait. Get started now!

# They're Watching

Yesterday I watched my team play. And, like the weather, the game turned cold and dreary. It was raining at the game and here. The conclusion of the game boiled down to a long shot for a field goal. Fifty-five yards, in the rain—practically impossible. Yet, somehow, the other team's kicker managed to split the uprights. The remaining seconds ticked away, taking my spirits with them. What a sinking, sickening feeling as we watched the victory and our team ranking slip away.

The cameras quickly turned from the game-winning field goal to our sidelines. They zoomed in on our coach. We wondered what his reaction would be to such a disappointing loss. It was almost as if he became another person. You could see the resignation to this disappointing reality as it washed over him. Yet, he sucked it up and began walking across the field. In the midst of his agony he congratulated the winning coach. We call that good sportsmanship. But in the deafening silence on the flight home, what do you do with all those emotions?

In the world outside of football, life is full of losses and heartaches as well. You were up for a promotion only to have the new guy snatch it away. Or maybe your teenager "borrows" the family car only to remodel it with an expensive dent to the front door panel. Your marriage isn't what you thought it would be. A friendship goes sour. Trust is betrayed. It's not a question of *if* losses will occur, but more of *when* they come into our lives. Knowing that challenges and difficulties are inevitable, how are we to deal with them when they do come?

Apparently, we're not the only ones struggling with life's disappointments. The first-century church needed encouragement too. James coached them to:

> Consider it a sheer gift, friends, when tests and challenges come at you from all sides. You know that under pressure, your faith-life is forced into the open and shows its true colors. So don't try to get out of anything prematurely. Let it do its work so you become mature and well-developed, not deficient in any way.
>
> James 1:2–4 (MSG)

This is certain: troubles are coming. You might not have a pack of cameras trained on you. But the people whom you influence? You can count on this: they're watching.

## Study the Playbook

**READ:** Romans 5:3–4;
2 Chronicles 15:7; 1 Corinthians 9:24

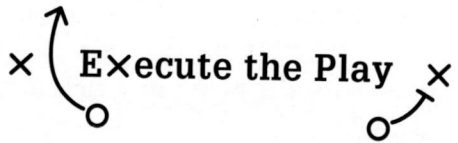

# Execute the Play

When you encounter a defeat or disappointment, it's crucial that you turn your focus onto God. Remind yourself of His agenda. Remind yourself that the same God Who is watching you is also in control. Remind yourself that He will cause you to be victorious, in the end!

_____

_____

_____

_____

_____

_____

_____

_____

_____

_____

_____

# Underrated and Unappreciated

rafted, played, traded, played, traded, played, traded—and so the NFL carousel goes. It finally ends when one team releases the athlete and the phone no longer rings with a new deal. The ride is over. Silence is deafening.

What happened? Talent was apparent. Your passion for the game ran full steam. Ability and finesse showed as you gave the game your all. Loyalty and team spirit coursed through your veins. You played their game by their rules. But just when you thought you were embracing success, they sent you packing. You were expendable. They needed another player who was more valuable to the team. "Nothing personal," is what they always said. "It's just business." How does that help? How do you explain to your family that it's time to move again?

The weights you press and the tackles you break attest to your strength. But in the silence of an empty locker room, their "business deals" scream rejection.

And all the strength-training in the league is never enough to shoulder the burden of such pain. Now what?

The agony of rejection is not unique to athletes. Think about the teen who is overlooked for the prom or the socialite who is never quite "polished enough" to belong. There is the son or daughter who can't achieve enough to win parental approval. Glance at the businessman who is bypassed for the latest promotion. And we sympathize with the "uncool" parent who is snubbed by her offspring. The scenarios vary, as do the levels of pain. Nonetheless, we all have had rejection carve its name in the halls of our hearts.

After bearing the brunt of numerous rejections, many of us fear that our heavenly Father will turn His back on us too. Sadly, we often judge God by life's experiences. But we have only to turn to His eternal Word to find lasting truth. Moses reminded all mankind that God's love is not conditional. His battle cry still rallies all who will heed its call.

"Be strong and of good courage, do not fear nor be afraid … for the Lord your God, He is the One Who goes with you. He will not leave nor forsake you" (Deuteronomy 31:6, NKJV).

Others might turn their back on us, but our loving Father never will.

## Study the Playbook

**READ:** 1 John 4:7–21; 1 Peter 5:7; John 3:16

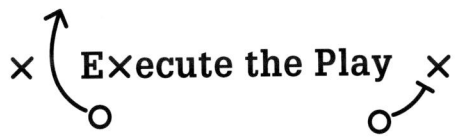

## Execute the Play

Print out Bible verses (like the ones listed) about God's love. When you feel rejected and unappreciated, read these verses out loud. Say them over and over, again. Do this until you remember that your heavenly Father loves you, and always will.

_____

_____

_____

_____

_____

_____

_____

_____

_____

_____

_____

_____

_____

_____

# Watch the X's and O's

O n Monday night and in every locker room, X's and O's represent a unique language: football. These little letters represent us versus the opponent, our team versus the adversary. For the fans, John Madden would use his yellow pen to break down the plays. In team meetings coaches illustrate how to outwit the opposition. The goal is to win—and always at the cost of the enemy.

As a child, X's and O's carried a totally different meaning. You remember getting Valentine cards in school and those birthday cards from your parents and grandparents. We all knew the XOXO's meant hugs and kisses.

To a couple, the X's and O's speak of a growing love and affection for the reader. Perhaps you signed love notes to your sweetheart in XOXO. With each new note and day, you were compelled to declare your love for your beloved. Finally, it was as clear to you both as it was to those around you. This precious relationship was designed for marriage.

The wedding day came. The bride was radiant and the groom proud. What a jubilant time! Celebration was in the air. The honeymoon was filled with bliss. Both were thrilled to be in each other's presence. Each lover studied the other with passion and peace. Yes, love was the language spoken here.

Time passed. It was filled with job interviews, bills, doctor's appointments, a baby, and numerous sleepless nights with the newborn. More time passed, bringing a work promotion, another baby, and more bills. Soccer games, piano lessons, and picking the children up from school soon dominated the schedule. As time moved on, a larger home was purchased and a job lay-off crashed in on this couple's parade. Bills piled up, as did more job-hunting and homework. Fatigue and an overflowing schedule marked the calendar.

Don't know when it happened or when they changed. But sometime in the midst of pushing through an existence, the X's and O's in the marriage turned from 'hugs and kisses' to 'me versus my opponent'. Sadly, more than 50 percent of all marriages end in divorce. What a staggering statistic! Yet, if we get so busy with life, our schedule can become our mistress and transform ultimately into a cruel master. There's a lesson to be learned here. Like the coach who brings us into the team meeting to study the X's and O's, we must be just as vigilant to watch our marital XOXO's. Here's the assignment: like a linebacker, find your target (of affection), wrap 'em up (in a loving embrace), and never let go.

"'For this reason a man will leave his father and mother and be united to his wife, and the two will become one flesh'? So they are no longer two, but one. Therefore what God has joined together, let man not separate" (Matthew 19:5–6).

## Study the Playbook

**READ:** Ephesians 5:31–33; Malachi 2:14–16; Colossians 3:12–17

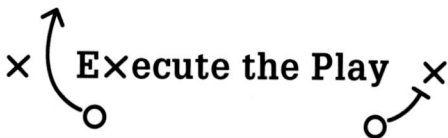

## E✕ecute the Play

Plan ahead and schedule weekly dates with your spouse. (Arrange for a highly qualified sitter for the children.) Plan outings that appeal to both of you. Look into each other's eyes, hold hands and reassure your beloved of your unconditional love.

_____

_____

_____

_____

_____

_____

# What Determines Excellence?

A while back our local team sent their premier running back, Julius Jones, to an autograph signing to help a store with its grand opening. Naturally, as a loyal fan, I was eager to meet him. My friend and I rushed off from work and headed to the mall for this special occasion.

Walking up to the store front, we were discouraged by the throng of people already waiting in line. To our further dismay, the security guard stepped in and announced the closing of the line and our opportunity. Perhaps the guard noticed the discouragement on our faces. He told us the line was closed but the store was open for business and we were free to go in and shop. With a new sense of purpose, we charged on into the store. It wasn't long before we had spotted our target. Fully aware that there would be no face-to-face conversation or any granting of an autograph, we were eager to secure the next best thing: a snapshot from the closest point possible.

Picture this: our RB was surrounded by his agent, security, store staff, and a steady stream of fans. It was beginning to look as if the possibility of a snapshot might be out of the question too. Not willing to accept defeat just yet, we asked the security detail if they would ask our star to look up for us. Thankfully, they were willing to oblige. In between autographs, he paused, looked up, and shot us a *Sports Illustrated* cover smile. Unfortunately, that attempt was marred with the passing of another security guard. Having come this close to our prize, we were unwilling to give up after one try. As the next fan passed through, there was a short lull and Julius looked directly at us, flashing his winning smile. Thrilled with our photo catch, we headed out.

You're probably thinking, *Hey, what's the big deal?* At first, I wondered too. But then I began to study the replays of this memory in my mind. I discovered a truth hiding beneath all the commotion. Julius was there to meet and sign autographs. He didn't have to do anything extra. But he did. He paid attention to the small things, like smiling for a disappointed fan to capture a valuable snapshot. You see, it's the attention to the small things that determines excellence. It's doing what's required plus a bit more that defines greatness.

Jesus taught this lesson through a parable. He explained how ten men were given an equal amount of investment. Out of the ten, the first was the most productive. The master commended him by saying, "Well done, good servant; because you were faithful in a very little, have authority over ten cities" (Luke 19:17, NKJV).

Now, you and I might not be punching holes to run for a game winning touchdown. But we can be faithful servants of our Master by paying attention to the small things in our lives and stretching out to excellence in all that we do.

## Study the Playbook

READ: Philippians 1:9–10;
2 Corinthians 8:7; 1 Corinthians 10:31

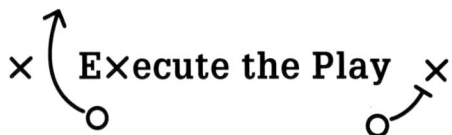 Execute the Play

When you're facing another dreaded chore, imagine a packed stadium. They're all there to watch you. In the Owner's box sits Jesus. Put all your energy into your task at hand. You will accomplish your task victoriously. Listen carefully…Jesus is cheering!

_____

_____

_____

_____

_____

# A License for Defiance?

**W**e see it demonstrated almost every game day. A star athlete doesn't get the play time or attention he thinks he rightly deserves. He flies off into a grownup version of a toddler's temper tantrum: jumping and stomping, throwing his helmet, or screaming at the coaches and officiating crew. What he hoped would be a frightening display of power is viewed as a ridiculous and shameful expression of selfishness and immaturity. Too often we give way and give in to these glory hogs of the gridiron. Since when should great talent be a license for defiance?

Fits of rebellion are not limited to the turf. Ask any public school teacher about the tenor of today's classroom. Tensions ride high as students regularly challenge the authority of not only the teachers but the administrators as well. What aggravates the problem is the growing number of parents (especially mommies) who insist on coddling and blindly defending their "gifted and faultless" offspring. Rebellion and anarchy also encircle the corporate break room much like hyenas as they drool over their trapped prey. Gossip and the character assassination of upper management create an environment of dissension. Disrespect coupled with disdain, wed in secrecy, are crucial elements in the birth of treason on any level.

Jealousy, lust, and a ravenous hunger for controlling power demand the overthrow of anything and any ruler standing in the way of self-gratification and glorification. Paul warned all peoples, past and present, that God will not tolerate any form of challenge to His power or purposes.

> The authorities that exist have been established by God. Consequently, he who rebels against the authority is rebelling against what God has instituted, and those who do so will bring judgment on themselves.
>
> Romans 13: 1b-2

In the end, whether the outcome is a game or school suspension, job termination or legal conviction, all those foolish enough to pursue personal glory by the pathway of rebellion will face some form of judgment. The ultimate glory hog, Lucifer, followed his demented passion for sovereignty. His treason cost him heaven. What will your rebellion cost you?

## Study the Playbook

READ: Isaiah 63:10; Psalm 107:10–12; Job 34:21–27

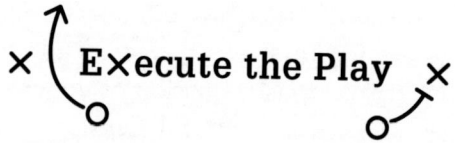

## Execute the Play

Are you struggling with submitting to the leadership of authorities? When you are given a directive that really rubs you the wrong way, picture Jesus as the one asking you to serve Him. Say yes to obedience. Give Jesus the key to unlocking blessings He has stored up for you.

# Building a House

**H**ave you ever built a house? If you have, you know what I'm talking about. It is such an undertaking. There are so many details: selection of brick, carpet, flooring, tile, backsplash, appliances, paint, etc. Weather conditions and shortages from the supply companies almost guarantee that the move-in date will be postponed several times. In a nutshell, the process is challenging, frustrating, and exciting all at the same time. So why do we do it? It is the promise of greatness to come.

Jerry Jones, the owner of the Dallas Cowboys, just built a "house" for his "boys." Now, you know everything in Texas is better because it's bigger. And this stadium is no exception. With a seating capacity of eighty thousand and the ability to accommodate up to 112,000 (through multiple standing areas), it has already housed the largest football audience ever.* The icing on this cake is its retractable roof. What an incredible sight!

With the excitement of building the new stadium came a great deal of anxiety. There was a sea of questions: would it be completed on time? would the work be performed to the highest levels of codes and standards? would they stay within the budget? You can relate to these doubts. But God taught us that if we want success in building, we must seek Him as our Master Builder (Psalm 127:1).

Do you ever find yourself anxious about the status of your eternal home? Perhaps you've wondered just where that might be and what you can expect. Jesus told His disciples:

> Believe in God, believe also in Me. In My Father's house are many mansions; if it were not so, I would have told you. I go to prepare a place for you…
> I will come again and receive you to Myself; that where I am, there you may be also.
>
> John 14:1–3 (NKJV)

If you know Christ as your personal Savior, then you have no reason to worry. He is your General Contractor, building a true dream home for you.

## Study the Playbook

READ: Psalm 34:10b; John 1:12; Romans 10:9–13

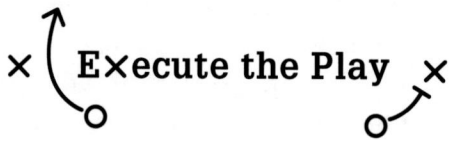

## Execute the Play

Do you ever doubt whether your salvation is secure? Did you receive Jesus as your Savior?

If you have, relax. Jesus has taken care of all the details. The next time you begin to worry, answer this question: Is His death on the cross enough proof of His love for you? Jesus paid the total price. There is NO outstanding balance. Your heavenly mansion will be waiting for you. Start thanking Him for this wondrous gift!

*Cowboys stadium seating capacity
http://sports.espn.go.com/travel/stadium/index?venue=nfl_6

_____

_____

_____

_____

_____

_____

_____

_____

_____

_____

_____

_____

# Carried Off the Field

There's an injury timeout on the field. Another player is down. It's every coach's nightmare, wife's and mother's fear, fan's dismay, and player's heartbreak. The game has stopped. All eyes zero in on the hurt athlete. His teammates come near. Bending down, they see the grimace of pain blanketing his face. He's not able to get up. The injury is too severe. It is more than his strength can bear. His two comrades reach down, scoop him in their arms, and carry him off the field in their human chair.

In that moment, God painted a picture to illustrate the Scriptures. "Stoop down and reach out to those who are oppressed. Share their burdens" (Galatians 6:2, MSG).

Very few of us will live in the world of football, but we all know those times when agonizing pain has taken us out of the game of life. It's not the daily challenges I'm talking about. No. Those God expects us to carry. But I am talking about those massive boulders of burden that would bury us if we had to bear them alone. There are those in our "own backyard" who are about to be crushed under too heavy of a load. A five year old little girl's mother dies of a rare disease. A father loses his job in a market that only has shut doors. An affair destroys another marriage. Addiction claims another life. These families are in our neighborhoods, schools, and churches. Regrettably, there is a cancer growing in the body of Christ. A common response to another's pain and hardships is a trite promise of prayer, a smile and a quick handshake. It's as if we're afraid of getting involved, that their heartaches might be contagious. This isn't the way our Lord intended His church to answer each other's needs. We must help them carry that overwhelming burden. Sometimes we feel unsure of how we can help. Mercy often comes clothed in practicality. You could bring a meal or send a gift card for a dinner delivered to their door. Maybe you can help with the yard work or chores around the house. Your way of helping might best come in the form of a listening ear, loving heart, and a strong shoulder to cry on. Perhaps you could pay the rent or next light bill. There are many ways to help. Here's what needs to be understood: There is no perfect way of helping to shoulder that burden. Don't let your fears get in the way of reaching out to one in need. Let God direct you on what is best. One thing is clear: don't walk away and leave your teammate on the field.

## Study the Playbook

READ: 1 John 3:17; Hebrews 13:16; James 2:14–17

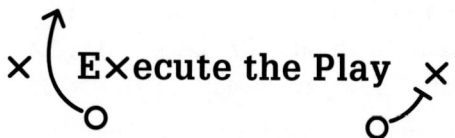

## Execute the Play

The next time the phone rings and your friend needs you, roll up your sleeves and reach out. Avoid trite platitudes. Be honest. Be open. Help in specific ways to meet genuine needs. If you don't know what to do, ask. Your friend will appreciate knowing that you're really willing to help out.

_____

_____

_____

_____

_____

_____

_____

_____

_____

_____

_____

# The Life of a Kicker

Signed, practiced with the team. Game day, made one field goal but missed a potentially game-winning kick. Released on Monday, picked up later that week by another team. And so the loop begins. Today's NFL kickers live in a constant time warp of an unending rewind. A dream or nightmare, but it's never quite living. How does it feel to live under such scrutiny? One minute, you're a part of the team; you belong. After the next kick, you're history.

You might not be in a football uniform, but you understand all too well what I'm talking about. You know that gnawing feeling of never being good enough to belong. Maybe it started with your parents. They let you know your behavior or grades were never quite good enough to earn their approval. Or it could be your spouse. You're not attractive or successful enough to win her love and devotion. Or it might be your boss who doesn't find you ambitious enough to keep you on the payroll. Have you become convinced that you will never be good enough? Just waiting for the other shoe to drop, aren't you?

It would be so easy to put God into that same box with your parents, boss, and spouse. There's just one problem: He doesn't fit. He knew we would come up against such odds in life. Our loving Father made it abundantly clear that His love for us could not be bought or stolen.

> Yes, I am sure that neither death, nor life, nor angels, nor ruling spirits, nothing now, nothing in the future, no powers, nothing above us, nothing below us, nor anything else in the whole world will ever be able to separate us from the love of God that is in Christ Jesus our Lord.
>
> Romans 8:38–39 (NCV)

When He declares His love for us, it is for all eternity. Missed field goals, poor grades, job layoffs, or any of our failures will never be able to stop God from loving us. No more getting kicked off the team! Now that's a winning score.

## Study the Playbook

READ: 2 Corinthians 1:21–22; Philippians 1:6; Ephesians 2:10

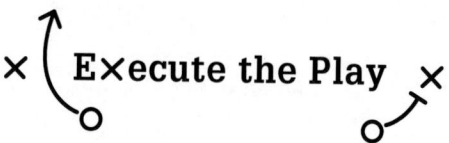

## Execute the Play

When you feel that everyone has given up on you, go back to God's word and see what He has to say about you. Quote aloud Bible verses that remind you that God is heavily invested into you. You can be certain; He wants you to succeed, because you are His child and creation.

# Fantasy Football

The name says it all. It's the game we love so much, except it's just an elaborate mirage. If you've ever played Fantasy Football, you know what it's all about. It starts with the draft. Be careful to choose your players wisely. It could cost you dearly during the season. And you have to pick your coaching staff just as wisely. They can make or break the team. It doesn't take long for it to seem like you're in the real world of professional football. What is fantasy is soon perceived as reality.

I encounter numerous people who find it perfectly acceptable to become immersed in a fantasy world of football, yet get quite offended when I invite them to come to a church service or Bible study. Here are some of the excuses I've heard:

- It's just for women and children.

- It's a crutch for those who are weak and need it.

- It's full of hypocrites.

- It's just fairytales and legends, like
  what I was told as a child.

Doesn't it seem odd that grown adults accept fantasy as reality, yet reject the ultimate reality as fantasy? Paul ran across similar issues with some of his contemporaries in Corinth. Here's what he had to say on that matter:

> Where is the wise person? Where is the educated person? Where is the skilled talker of this world? God has made the wisdom of the world foolish ... But God chose the foolish things of the world to shame the wise, and he chose the weak things of the world to shame the strong. He chose what the world thinks is unimportant and what the world looks down on and thinks is nothing in order to destroy what the world thinks is important. God did this so that no one can brag in his presence.
>
> 1 Corinthians 1:20, 27–29 (NCV)

The challenges of yesterday and today are the same. Will we gamble to believe that the Bible is just some elaborate children's bedtime storybook, or will we dare to believe God and His love are real? It's the bet of a lifetime. Be extremely careful. It just might be yours that's at stake.

## Study the Playbook

**READ:** Revelation 3:20; John 3:1–21

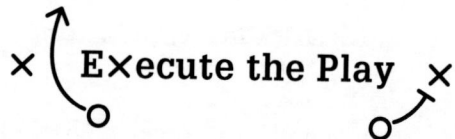

## Execute the Play

You've probably grown up hearing about Jesus all your life. But this story seemed too simple to be valid. Stop allowing others to determine what you think and believe. Investigate Jesus. Discover if He truly is Who He claims to be. Then choose to decide Who He will be to you.

---

---

---

---

---

---

---

---

---

---

---

---

---

---

# Offense versus Defense

**W**hich is more important, the offense or the defense? Actually, it's a trick question. Both are equally important when your team is playing. Without either one, the game would result in either an immediate forfeit or a devastating loss.

The strain between the two sides of the ball is not an uncommon problem in the game of football. Different coaches and teams have created a variety of ways to deal with the problem. Nonetheless, the ego-driven issue persists.

This problem is not unique to the world of football, though. You've probably seen children fussing with their siblings. Or maybe you have fallen prey to arguing with your spouse over who has the most important role in the family. Why is it that we find ourselves in conflict with others regarding how significant we are? We can take some solace in the fact that this struggle isn't new. Paul talked with the Corinthians about this same issue. They had become caught

up in a debate over whose gifts, and therefore which persons, were more valuable. Paul answered:

> The body is not one member but many … God has set the members, each one of them, in the body just as He pleased. And if they were all one member, where would the body be? But now indeed there are many members, yet one body … the members should have the same care for one another. And if one suffers, all the members suffer with it; or if one member is honored, all the members rejoice with it.
>
> 1 Corinthians 12:14, 18–20, 25–26 (NKJV)

In conclusion, there isn't any need for debate. Each position, role, and most importantly, each person is uniquely significant. Each must be in place, fully functioning, for the team/family to be effective. Let me encourage you: the next time you feel the need to negate another's importance in order to exalt yours, resist that urge. Instead, rejoice in your differences and cheer on your teammate to a joint victory in Christ.

## Study the Playbook

**READ:** James 3:13–18;
1 Corinthians 3:1–3; Romans 13:8, 10

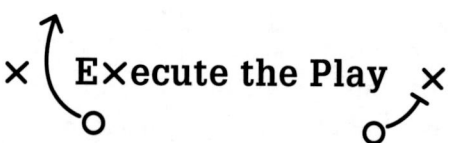

## Execute the Play

While you might have to compete with someone to earn a position on your job, that is *not* the case with your church or family. Choose to recognize the good in every family member. Give sincere praise as it is genuinely earned. Say goodbye to jealousy!

_____

_____

_____

_____

_____

_____

_____

_____

_____

_____

_____

_____

_____

_____

_____

_____

_____

# Going, Going, Gone

I t's amazing how often players find themselves on the go. Team meetings, practices, rehab sessions, appointments with the team doctors, PR events, giving back to the community through service, and flying out of town for away games—the list of demands seems unending. Pretty soon these players find that they have little remaining for themselves. Oftentimes, what the player brings home are leftovers of energy and emotions. Too much of this scenario and it leaves the family with emotional bruises and injuries that would rival those after a tough, post-season game. Over time, some wives decide that they can't keep up the façade. They walk away from the game and their marriage, leaving behind a stunned and wounded soldier.

"He should have seen it coming."

"He should have invested more time into his marriage and family."

"What with all the away games, he was probably having some kind of extramarital activity on the side."

"It's his own fault. He made his bed. Now he's got to sleep in it."

These and many other malicious accusations are hurled in the man's direction. From the safety of anonymity, it's rather easy to sit back and judge "these poor suckers" for their indulgences, ignorance, and incompetence. The problem with pointing a finger at someone else is that it leaves three fingers pointing back at yourself. So, what if the world were to take an investigating look at our investment into our marriage and family? How would we stack up? How would our spouses and children answer that question?

Anyone can build a house, but it takes maturity and sacrifice to build a home. Jesus warned that we are to weigh the investment costs before beginning; otherwise it can leave us as the laughingstock of the community (Luke 14:28–30). Before we allow broken hearts and shattered dreams to auction off our family, let's be careful to invest in our most prized possession: our family.

> Suppose one of you wants to build a tower. Will he not first sit down and estimate the cost to see if he has enough money to complete it? For if he lays the foundation and is not able to finish it, everyone who sees it will ridicule him, saying, "This fellow began to build and was not able to finish."
>
> Luke 14:28–30

# Study the Playbook

READ: Genesis 2:18, 21–24;
Ephesians 5:25–29; 1 Peter 3:7

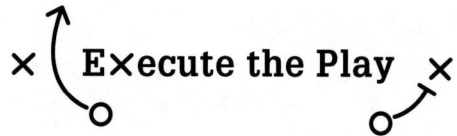

## Execute the Play

Men, you must be intentional in continuing to pursue your wife, just like you did when you were first courting. Plan weekly dates. Give her days off, where she can be "just a lady". This may mean that you clean the house and take care of the children. Encourage her to take some time for herself. Maybe you can surprise her with a gift card for a pedicure and a trip to the hair salon. Remind her just how beautiful she is to you … still.

_____

_____

_____

_____

_____

_____

_____

_____

_____

_____

# He Shows Up

Just like they do every year, in 2005, many of the loyal and true joined together at the Cowboy's Season Kickoff Luncheon. While introducing Jason Witten, the recipient of the Offensive Player of the Year award, one of the local sports broadcasters, Babe Laughenburg, brought an interesting thought to mind. He described Jason as a player who 'shows up'. Now, in corporate America, just showing up wouldn't be enough to keep your parking space. But in the world of football, that phrase means something totally different. To show up means that the athlete gives his all, plus 10 percent more. It describes strength of character, integrity, and a strong work ethic that brings the respect of many.

The Old Testament boasts of such a man. Daniel was a man who did all that was required of him and more. His desire was to do everything necessary in order to demonstrate the excellence of the living God he served. Daniel obeyed God with courage and showed respect and honor to those in authority.

Could these same attributes be said of you or me? Keep in mind, Daniel was surrounded by close friends who also shared his passion for excellence and obedience. Daniel had three close friends who were willing to die in order to keep true to their faith. Do those in your closest circle demonstrate a similar level of faith, courage, and integrity?

Perhaps we too should follow suit and wisely select such champions to be our teammates in life. God bless you as you seek out others who burn with passion for God's truths and excellence.

> But Daniel resolved not to defile himself with the royal food and wine, and he asked the chief official for permission not to defile himself this way … "Please test your servants for ten days: Give us nothing but vegetables to eat and water to drink. Then compare our appearance with that of the young men who eat the royal food, and treat your servants in accordance with what you see." So he agreed to this and tested them for ten days. At the end of the ten days they looked healthier and better nourished than any of the young men who ate the royal food.
>
> Daniel 1:8, 12–15

# Study the Playbook

**READ:** Ecclesiastes 9:10a;
Romans 12:1; 2 Corinthians 9:6–7

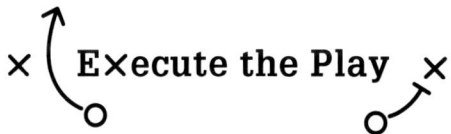

## Execute the Play

It's awfully hard for others to take you seriously when you give praise to God one minute but then the next moment you get recognized while drunk and out clubbing. Living for Christ may require some serious and costly sacrifices. You may have to give up some activities. And you might have to pick a new group of friends. But it will be worth it. Remember, everything valuable comes at a price.

# I Never Would Have Thought

The off-season is always full of surprises. Teams pick up free agents, scout out, and scoop up early round draft picks as well as release a few players. It's standard fare in the NFL. There are some players, however, who are staples, part of the team's foundation, if you will. These are the ones who we just assume are immune from release. I never would have thought that the Cowboys would have released Larry Allen. A nine-time pro-bowler and one of the best in the NFL, *LA* and *left guard for the Dallas Cowboys* have been synonymous terms. Fans and many within the hallowed halls of football thought the Lone Star had been permanently tattooed on this man. We just knew he would always be a part of the Cowboys roster.

What caused this change of heart for the Cowboys' front office? Maybe it was a coach weary of striving with temperamental outbursts. Or it might have been an owner tired of anteing up even more money for another contract holdout. It could have been a question of a player's increasing age colliding with the need to build the team's future. Perhaps it was really a case of trying to fit within the salary cap. We might never really know. But the truth still stands. Larry Allen is out of a star. Who would have thought?

Perhaps the feeling is similar to the man who stands dumbfounded when served divorce papers. Clueless and numb, he never saw it coming. Broken, he wonders what led up to such a revelation of rejection. What about the child who stands alone in the courthouse, having just heard the judge's decision to grant his parent's request to disown him? Crushed and bewildered, he can only wonder what he did to deserve such a sentence of abandonment. Both cry out in dismay, "Is any relationship true? Is any trust held sacred?"

Does your heart ache from wounds of rejection and abandonment? Do you too wonder if there is anyone who stands true to promises made, one whose love lasts? I have good news for you, friend. There is One.

"The LORD himself goes before you and will be with you; he will never leave you nor forsake you. Do not be afraid; do not be discouraged" (Deuteronomy 31:8).

Jesus knew that you and I would carry broken hearts and shattered dreams. He knew that we wouldn't be able to believe yet another promise after having lived in the wake of so many empty ones. He knew we would need some type of proof. And that's exactly what Jesus did. He proved that His love was true. He nailed His promise to Calvary's tree.

# Study the Playbook

**READ:** Jeremiah 29:11–14; John 10:10

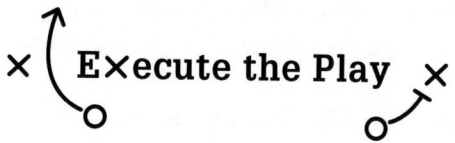

## Execute the Play

You feel rejected and discouraged. Now is a good time to remember that God is still in control. Read these verses out loud. Every time your emotions begin to spiral downward, remind yourself that God has an incredible plan, full of blessings, waiting for you!

_____

_____

_____

_____

_____

_____

_____

_____

_____

_____

# Live and On-air

Two of the greatest the sports broadcasting industry has ever known: Al Michaels and John Madden. Their job has been to tell us what they see, hear, and know. They've reported the facts and stats, personal tidbits, and injury reports. Their description of the stadium, weather, mood of the fans, and their break down of the plays gives us the feel of the game from an insider's point of view.

These two men have reported the game in such a way that it makes me wish I was there—not just as a fan, but playing the game with the best the league has to offer. It becomes so real that I want to be in the very middle of all the action. With the excitement of the game and their expert skills in reporting, I'm not tempted to reach for the remote.

Our Christian lifestyle should mimic Al and John's job description. We are to report all that God has done (and is doing) in our lives to those who are watching and listening to us. Feel a bit uncomfortable doing that? Jesus said to "go ... and tell all that God has done for you" (Luke 8:39, HCSB).

We are to help others see the Christian life in such an appealing and fulfilling way that they wouldn't dream of grabbing life's remote to surf to another channel. Here's how we do this.

1. We gather our stats (read the Bible) before the game (meeting up with those seeking to know God).

2. We study the players and coaches. (We know Jesus, God, and heroes of the faith through consistent Bible study.)

3. We familiarize ourselves with the locale and its fans. (Spend time to develop friendships with those seeking the truth. Get to know their interests, likes, and needs.)

4. We have our information, mikes, and sound equipment set up. (Remember and rehearse all the good things God has done for you.)

The music introduces the game, and we're on-air. With the clock ticking and the cameras rolling, it's time to tell the good news: Jesus loves everyone, and His salvation is free for the asking.

## Study the Playbook

**READ:** Matthew 28:18–20; 1 Timothy 4:13–16

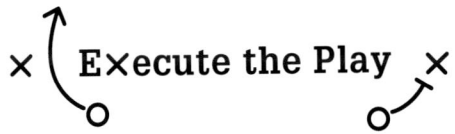

## Execute the Play

Join a local Bible study so you can grow and mature. Read your Bible daily. Pray and ask God for Him to "coach you up" on what you read. Purchase some witnessing tracts to share with others. Live a life of excellence. Tell others about Christ every time the opportunity presents itself.

_____
_____
_____
_____
_____
_____
_____
_____
_____
_____
_____
_____

# Measure Up

I t's Pro Day at the college campus. All the eligible players for the upcoming draft are brought before the media and scouts. They are weighed. Their height is taken. The length of each man's arms is measured. The judges record the speed of this athlete's forty-yard dash, the height of his standing jump, and every other possible drill and test the player can be put through.

Quite honestly, the whole circus reminds me of our local stock show. The prized animal is paraded in the center show ring before the throngs of bidders. It has been weighed, measured, and tagged. How well it shows determines who will purchase it and what price will be paid.

How many of us feel as if we are in some type of arena, being shown to the crowds? What anxiety we experience as we strive to be perfect while we are put through a series of tests and jump through a set of hoops! All this dog and pony show just to see if we measure up.

This generation seems to be filled with people who have grown up with a performance-based mindset. It

goes something like this: "If I perform well enough (on whatever task is set before me), I might earn the approval of those who are important. And if I succeed in winning their approval, then I am significant." This pathetic portrait doesn't stop here. Those who are caught up in this mindset believe that God fits in with the rest of these judges too. Do you find yourself buying into the belief that you must somehow measure up to God's standards and expectations in order to win His approval? Tragic as it might be, too many of us have.

Is our significance truly tied to our performance? Thankfully, God is not silent. We learn that "God put His love on the line for us by offering His Son in sacrificial death while we were of no use whatever to Him" (Romans 5:8, MSG). We have further reassurance when God says, "I've never quit loving you and never will. Expect love, love and more love," (Jeremiah 31:3, MSG). According to God's Word, there is no basis for a faulty belief system. We don't have to measure up to win His love and approval, not now nor ever. God's blessing: our relief.

## Study the Playbook

READ: John 15:16; Psalm 34:10b; Psalm 27:14

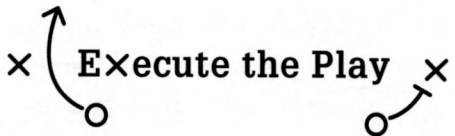

## Execute the Play

Every time you feel like you aren't worthy of being loved, read aloud Jeremiah 31:3. Stop replaying failures from your past. Choose to focus on the good and growth that God is bringing into your life.

_____

_____

_____

_____

_____

_____

_____

_____

_____

_____

_____

_____

_____

_____

_____

# Playing in the Past?

t was my team's final game of the season. I watched with mixed feelings. It was good to see a losing season come to an end. What a disappointment! But it wasn't supposed to play out that way. In fact, at the beginning of the season, there had been hopeful whispers of playoffs and some of us even dared to dream of another trip to the Super Bowl.

Across the state you could hear people questioning what went wrong. Not to be left out I had my pocketful of theories as well. It could have been that our beloved coach was trying to recreate glory days of the past. He had set up the team roster with some of those same players. Yes, they've been some of the best the league has ever seen. Notice the emphasis on the past tense. How can we build a future when we're still holding on to the past? Our season never reached the *present* because we were too busy trying to recreate the *past.* So how can we possibly build a team of the *future?*

With the season over, the players got a much-needed rest. But the coaches and owner began the tedious task of burning the midnight oil. I hope they weren't imprisoned with what-if questions, that only serve to condemn and stymie any progress. Instead, I hope they chose to ask the important questions : *What will it take to earn a winning season? How do we get there? What changes must we embrace? What sacrifices must be made? What good-byes must be said?*

As we enter the New Year, some of us might assess the previous year as a losing season. Could it be that we've been too busy living in the past, trying to recreate what *was* rather than what *is*? What's the problem in doing this? If it resulted in victory before, then why can't we just keep repeating a winning formula? Here are some thoughts: 1) players age and can lose some of their quality of play; and 2) defenses become familiar with our offense.

A lot of life's lessons mirror those from the gridiron. We age, and lose some of our "edge"; circumstances are always changing. If we stay trapped in the past, we can almost guarantee a "losing season". For the sake of present and future victories, we must release the agonies of past losses as well as the glories of yesterday's triumphs. We must begin the process of playing in the present. It's the greatest game day yet.

"One thing I do: forgetting what is behind and straining toward what is ahead, I press on toward the goal to win the prize for which God has called me heavenward in Christ Jesus" (Philippians 3:13–14).

## Study the Playbook

READ: 2 Corinthians 5:17; Romans 8:1; Isaiah 43:18–19; Lamentations 3:22–23

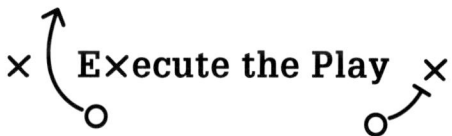

## Execute the Play

Whether you bombed or scored the winning touchdown, yesterday is over. Concentrate on the new day God has given to you. Follow His direction to create an agenda to accomplish His new goals for you.

_____

_____

_____

_____

_____

_____

_____

_____

_____

_____

_____

_____

_____

# Retiring from the Game

**E**very year some of the top stars in the NFL retire from the game. They call a press conference in which they express their gratitude to their coaches, family, friends, and fans. It is usually an emotional time for the player and those watching.

Case in point: who can ever forget the poignant goodbye Emmitt Smith gave to the game he's loved so long and well? At the press conference, he clutched his bride Patricia's hand and tucked it into his chest as securely as he used to carry the ball. A strong and passionate man, he allowed us a brief glimpse into his soul. His grief was real and raw as he gave his final goodbye to his life and dream of football. We were thankful that he allowed us to share in that tender but gut-wrenching moment.

How heartbreaking it can be to witness a player retiring from the game. Yet, it is a necessary part of life. There is sorrow as we close a chapter in life. On the other hand, it paves the way for new joys, as we are then freed to walk into a new chapter. We witnessed such an event as we mourned the passing of Coach Tom Landry. What a godly man. What a legacy he has given to the game. We would have kept him for all time, but he received a call to go home. Just as he was on the sidelines, he quietly retired from the game of life. We knew that that day must come. Paul made this truth very clear when he wrote, "It is appointed for men to die once" (Hebrews 9:27, NKJV).

Somewhere in heaven, Coach Landry is strolling along with the Master. One day, you and I will have to retire from the game of life, too. It is my heart's greatest desire that I will see you that day, in our Father's house.

> In my Father's house are many rooms; if it were not so, I would have told you. I am going there to prepare a place for you. And if I go and prepare a place for you, I will come back and take you to be with me that you also may be where I am.
>
> John 14:2–3

# Study the Playbook

**READ:** Revelation 21:4;
Romans 6:23; Ecclesiastes 12:7

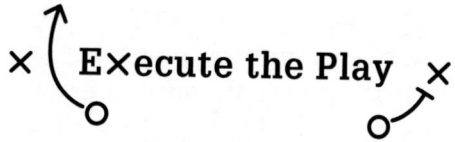

## Execute the Play

Death will eventually come for us all. You need to have a plan for your retirement from the game of life. Contact your attorney and create a will. Save some of your income so that you can create an inheritance for your children. Set aside funds to cover funeral and burial expenses. Most importantly, book your permanent stay in Heaven by receiving Christ as your Savior!

_____

_____

_____

_____

_____

_____

_____

_____

_____

_____

# Someone, Please Stop the Bleeding

**W**atching from the stands, it was one of those games during which you begin to feel sorry for the other team. The home team was walloping the would-be contenders. By the third quarter, the visiting team was beginning to hemorrhage. I couldn't help but wonder if their coach was crying out, "Someone, please stop the bleeding!" It was the game clock that ended up coming to the rescue. The final tick had passed, and the game was now history. With a final score of 82–38, it was clear that this team was D.O.A.

Hop in a time machine and warp back two thousand years. You find yourself amidst a raucous crowd. But it's a totally different scene. You flinch. You just got splattered with something wet. Looking down, you see that it's blood. More than curious, you're anxious to find whose blood you're wearing. It's a man, or at least you think so. This person has been beaten so badly that he's past recognition. He groans under His heavy load. His pain is unbearable, yet He struggles on through this nightmarish journey. For a brief moment, He turns to look at you. Your eyes lock. All at once, you've been ushered into eternity. You know this man. All His pain begins to swell over you. Looking heavenward, you scream, "Someone, please stop the bleeding!"

Slip back to the here and now. Even still, you hear a soft answer. God's Holy Spirit whispers to you, "Without the shedding of blood, there is no forgiveness of sins" (Hebrews 9:22, NLT).

Jesus had to die for us to live (John 3:16–17, 10:10). He was and is the only way to our heavenly Father (John 14:6). Thankfully, the bleeding has stopped. Please don't waste a drop of His blood. Receive His gift of life and *live!*

## Study the Playbook

**READ:** 1 Peter 3:18; 1 Corinthians 15:22; 1 John 2:2

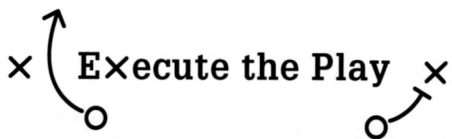

### Execute the Play

This moment is all you have that is certain. If you have not received Christ as your Savior, do that now. Tomorrow may be too late.

# Terriers and Wide Receivers

My daughter has a little dog named Dinky. He's a terrier mix. For all you dog lovers, you know that means he thinks he's a Rottweiler. Some of you are reading this and chuckling. You have a terrier too? Others of you are reading this and wondering what this "cute" little conversation has to do with football. Hang on to your cleats. I'm getting there. Here's my point: Terriers and wide receivers both have BDS—big dog syndrome. Wide receivers are the terriers of the field. They believe they can take on anything and anyone at any time.

Think of some of the prominent wide outs of the game.

"Give me the ball."

"I'm wide open."

"I'm *The* Playmaker. Just get me the ball."

These statements reflect the player's all out drive to win: one hundred percent, giving it all he's got. This admirable level of confidence and commitment is just the attitude every coach wants from all his team.

Unfortunately, somewhere down the path of his career, the player often lets this commitment get twisted and distorted. He begins to think the team can't win or survive without him. He begins to think of himself as a demigod. He begins to see what others can do to serve him. All those blessed with greatness must be on guard against such an insidious attack of pride. Paul had to caution the Christians in Rome and Philippi.

"I give each of you this warning: Be honest in your estimate of yourselves" (Romans 12:3, NLT).

"Don't be selfish; don't live to make a good impression on others. Be humble, thinking of others as better than yourself" (Philippians 2:3, NLT).

These lessons fly in the face of all that our culture teaches.

You don't have to be a terrier or a wide receiver to be great. As a believer, you have been called to greatness. In order to be truly great, you must "humble yourselves under the mighty hand of God, that He may exalt you in due time" (1 Peter 5:6, NKJV).

Rise to the top by staying on your knees.

## Study the Playbook

READ: James 4:6; Colossians 3:12; Proverbs 22:4

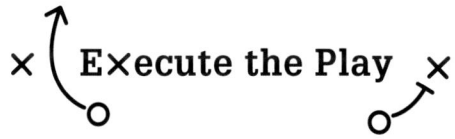

## Execute the Play

The easiest way to exalt God is to make a list of all His wonderful attributes. Be a spiritual color commentator: praise God for all He is. Don't stop there. Thank Him for all He does!

_____

_____

_____

_____

_____

_____

_____

_____

_____

_____

_____

_____

_____

_____

# Offside

If you want to see a head coach blow a fuse, just let any of his players jump offside and you'll catch the red-faced reaction. Here's the problem: the players have been coached too thoroughly for this type of amateurish mistake to occur. In a press conference following a game filled with too many of these penalties, Coach Parcells shook his head in confusion and disgust. He explained how frustrating it was to watch professionals continue making these mental mistakes. His point: all the player has to do is to keep his eye on the ball and keep his ear tuned to the audible. Only when the ball moves are any of the players to cross the line. Otherwise, a penalty is sure to be called.

It's frustrating for all of us to watch. But before we come down too hard on these guys, let's take a look at it from the player's perspective. They've been trained to beat their opponent off the line. That split second can mean the difference between a successfully completed play or a crunching sack. In an attempt to get to the ball our athlete jumps offside. Yes, he's in the right place but at the wrong time. No matter the intent, he rushed the play, and it resulted in a penalty. His impatience brought about a consequence that negatively affected him and the entire team.

In real life the same is true. Let's take the example of a romantic relationship. It's clear the couple is "meant for each other." They have declared their love for one another and have announced their engagement. To promote victory, they have been coached to keep their focus on Christ and listen to His audible to remain pure until their wedding night. Yet, in a moment of passion, someone crosses the line. What would be the right thing is wrong because it is before its time. The couple's impatience can bring on consequences that penalize them as well as family members and friends.

Even though there are repercussions due to their choices, unlike football, God gives grace and mercy. He can restore what has been stolen or broken. Our Lord offers forgiveness but requires the couple move on without further sin (John 8:1–11). Have you jumped offside? Don't despair. The game isn't lost. Accept the responsibility for your actions, stand strong in your commitment to purity, and press on toward a new victory in Christ.

> It is God's will that you should be sanctified: that you should avoid sexual immorality; that each of you should learn to control his own body in a way that is holy and honorable, not in passionate lust like the heathen, who do not know God.
>
> 1 Thessalonians 4:3–5

# Study the Playbook

**READ:** 1 Corinthians 6:18;
Galatians 5:13; Romans 6:11–14

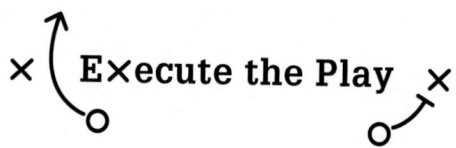

## Execute the Play

Before you start dating that special person, predetermine what steps you will take in order to protect moral purity for both of you. Arrange for your times together to be in public places, such as a restaurant, concert, game, church, etc. Plan ahead what time you will end the date and return home, ALONE! Have a trusted friend hold you accountable for how you act on and treat your date.

# The Cost of a Six-pack

**W**alk into your grocery store and check out the cost of your favorite soft drink six-pack. What motivates us to pay for these six packs is their sweet taste and a kick of energy.

Walk into any football locker room. The players come in from a hard workout or a tough game. Hot and sweaty, they start peeling out of their uniforms. Standing around in their shorts or towels, many reveal a hard, chiseled six-pack. Those didn't come cheap. For most, it's been a lifestyle of discipline and relentless hours of strenuous workouts in the gym. Paul could relate with the struggle of paying such a hefty price.

"I discipline my body like an athlete, training it to do what it should" (1 Corinthians 9:27a, NLT).

It's all about the price. What motivates an athlete to pay the price for his six-pack? It's a quality insurance against injury. The longer he can play injury free, the more renewed contracts come his way, and the greater his bank account.

Look at the graduate. What motivates the student to pay the price of hours of studying? A diploma and the hope of a financially bright future are the driving force.

Drop in on a couple's twenty-fifth anniversary celebration. What motivates this pair to pay the high cost of hammering out differences and heartaches? The look of lasting love in the other's eyes is the rewarding bait for a lifetime.

Anything in life that has great value has a lofty price tag attached. Whether it is a successful career in the NFL, the business world, family relationships, or service to the Lord, those who persevere find the cost worth paying. Paul had the same experience. He told the Christians at Philippi, "I strain to reach the end of the race and receive the prize for which God, through Christ Jesus, is calling us up to heaven" (Philippians 3:14, NLT).

Friend, be encouraged. Pull out the wallet of your soul, for the prize is worth the price.

## Study the Playbook

**READ:** 2 Timothy 2:15; Matthew 7:7–11; 1 John 5:14–15; Philippians 1:6

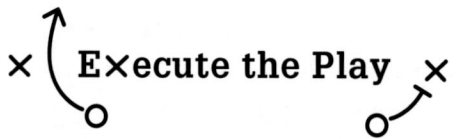

## Execute the Play

Follow these steps to win your prize. Think before you speak or act. Seek out godly people to advise you. Gather information so you are well informed. Surround yourself with people of high moral integrity who will encourage and hold you accountable to achieve your goals.

# They're All Alike

You've been talking with a group when the discussion turns to the latest football scandals in the papers. It isn't too long before someone is raking the whole league over the coals. Indictments and judgments are ruthlessly thrown around.

"They're all a bunch of overpaid, spoiled thugs."

"Womanizing drug addicts, the whole lot of them."

"They're just dumb brutes who can't do anything more than entertain the masses."

These are some pretty cruel and harsh statements. What makes these words so dangerous is how they reflect the heart and mind of the speaker.

Interesting how one bad apple spoils the whole barrel, isn't it? A teacher has an affair with a student. Suddenly, all teachers are vile. A lawyer skews the case. Now, all lawyers are corrupt. A minister molests a member from the congregation. Immediately, all clergy are sexual perverts. A politician siphons off money from public funds to his personal account. Instantly, all politicians are lying, greedy, power-hungry mongrels.

See how easy it is to judge and condemn? Notice how quickly this becomes a mindset? Like a barracuda, a critical spirit is ready to rip into the next group of losers. Some have reached such a depth of hardheartedness that they enjoy shredding others apart with their words. This kind of vicious behavior was prevalent when Jesus walked the earth. He warned all who would listen:

"Don't judge other people, and you will not be judged. Don't accuse others of being guilty, and you will not be accused of being guilty. Forgive, and you will be forgiven" (Luke 6:37, NCV).

I don't know about you, but I choose to listen to our Lord's warning. I would much rather receive His mercy than His judgment (Luke 6:36). And you? Which will you choose?

## Study the Playbook

READ: John 7:24; Ephesians 4:29;
Luke 6:31; Galatians 5:14

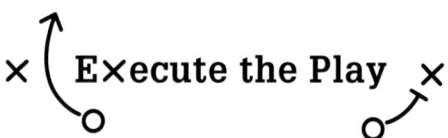

## Execute the Play

Before you criticize another, think of all your faults and past failures. Now, think of how many second chances you have received from others, and God. Remind yourself this person needs grace and mercy as well.

# Upended

What a phenomenal play. The wide receiver had grand plans on taking the ball into the end zone. Just inches away and the cornerback literally upended the wide-out. Talk about seeing the game from a different perspective. Upside down on the way to the turf makes for quite a jarring end to what was supposed to have been a glorious celebration.

How many times have you found yourself in a similar situation? You have grand, even godly plans, for resounding success only to find yourself in the midst of chaos, calamity, and confusion. You were thinking ahead to the children's college education, retirement, and basking in the sun on those cruises so long denied. And then a pink slip comes along and dashes those dreams against the jagged rocks of disappointment. Maybe you were painting the nursery and assembling the tiny furniture, hopefully awaiting the birth of your firstborn. And then a brutal sonogram reveals that your precious little one has already gone to be with the Lord. You were signed to a large and lengthy contract, looking ahead to a record-breaking career. And then a bone-crushing tackle takes you out of the game, the season, or even your career.

A piercing question swells up in the face of such adversity. Where is God when life paints a picture of pain? David wondered the very same thing. He knew that God had great plans for him. But here he was, supposed to be king; yet he was fleeing from his own son, Absalom. Talk about confusion and discouragement. David was dealing with a heavy dose of both.

"My tears have been my food day and night, while men say to me all day long, 'Where is your God?'" (Psalm 42:3).

What are we to do when we are overwhelmed by adversity and pain? It's simple but not easy. Go back to what you know. Remember what God has told you to do. Trust what He has promised you. We know that God is the same yesterday, today, and tomorrow (Hebrews 13:8). He keeps His promises. Stick to the game plan. You may be upended for a time, but in the end you will land standing tall.

## Study the Playbook

**READ:** Hebrews 11:1; Romans 15:13; Isaiah 40:31

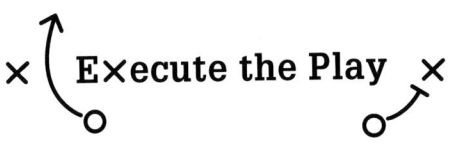

When your spirit is wounded and you feel defeated, fight the temptation to isolate. Seek out and spend time with mature Christians who will comfort and encourage you. Write down and quote Scriptures about hope and encouragement.

_____

_____

_____

_____

_____

_____

_____

_____

_____

_____

_____

_____

_____

_____

_____

_____

# We Salute You

He won the Outland Trophy his senior year with the Air Force Academy Falcons. Upon graduating from the academy, he served as an Air Force pilot of the A-10 Thunderbolt, flying forty-five missions in four years (in Iraq). Coming home, having been drafted in the eleventh round of the 1988 NFL Draft by the Dallas Cowboys, he entered as a twenty-seven-year-old rookie. For the next nine seasons, he went on to collect impressive stats but, most importantly, win three super bowl rings. Chad Hennings, we salute you.

December 7, 1941. Another American patriot. Just barely eighteen years old, this boy (along with the rest of his shipmates) warped into manhood as World War II exploded on America. Years of steadfast service stretched to the rank of lieutenant commander before an honorable medical discharge. An American hero, my daddy, William T. Bassett. We salute you.

Called by God to fight for His people. City after city, like Jericho, they were destroyed (Joshua 24:11). This man was God's appointed warrior to wipe out degradation and restore God's righteousness. Faithful and true, Joshua, we salute you.

A former skeptic, a relentless persecutor, a brilliant scholar, a man of means and influence, a passionate preacher—God called this powerful orator to win nations to Christ (Ephesians 3:8). A martyr for his Master, Paul, we salute you.

An Air Force pilot, a Navy shipman, an Old Testament warrior, a New Testament evangelist, the face in your mirror—all have been given their orders. We are to put on our issued uniform (Ephesians 6:11) and fight the good fight (1 Timothy 6:12). On that day when we are honorably discharged from our tour of duty on earth, may God Almighty and His holy army look at us and say, "We salute you" (Luke 19:17).

> "I have fought the good fight, I have finished the race, I have kept the faith" (2 Timothy 4:7 NCV).

## Study the Playbook

**READ:** Philippians 4:13;
Romans 8:28–29; Matthew 25:23

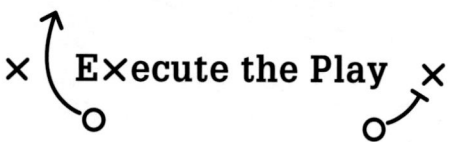

## Execute the Play

Before you go to bed, have your "orders" for tomorrow written down. Each day, have a plan to reach the mark God has given to you. Never give up. Be diligent. Keep fighting until you win!

I would like to honor all our military men
and women, past and present, who have
served to make our country great and free.

_____

_____

_____

_____

_____

_____

_____

_____

_____

_____

_____

_____

_____

_____

_____

_____

# What If?

Recently, during the game the coach was lobbying to get time added back onto the game clock. Here's the situation that led up to that decision. One of the officials had thrown the yellow flag. After he and the rest of the officiating team huddled for a micro-conference, they decided there was no penalty on the play after all. But they had forgotten to reset the game clock to put the erroneously lost time back onto the clock. The livid coach was screaming to regain those lost seconds, threatening to throw his red flag to gain their attention. They heard his call and were able to comply. It had been an honest mistake. Fortunately the officials were able to set it right by putting those few seconds back on the clock.

Maybe you're thinking it strange that a coach was ready to pop a blood vessel over a few lost seconds. But if you're like the majority of Americans, you're also struggling with a day that's constantly too short. Day after day, you've got twenty-six hours of scheduling that you're trying to squeeze into twenty-four. Have you wondered, what if there were more hours in your day? You're not alone. Too many of us have crammed into the ship of over-commitment and busyness. I have good news for you. There is relief for getting out of this whirlwind lifestyle. God has a plan.

"The steps of a good man are ordered by the Lord, and He delights in his way" (Psalm 37:23, NKJV).

God wants order in our daily schedule. Take a look at His day timer (Ecclesiastes 3) and you'll get an idea of how He organizes and prioritizes life. God wants us to stop stressing out over our schedules. Jesus taught, "You cannot add any time to your life by worrying about it" (Matthew 6:27, NCV).

Our Master gave us a limited amount of time and wants us to learn how to use it wisely for His glory and His purposes.

"The thing you should want most is God's kingdom and doing what God wants. Then all these other things you need will be given to you" (Matthew 6:33, NCV).

Let's stop playing the what-if game of more time. Instead, let's live and enjoy God's gift to us: the present.

## Study the Playbook

READ: 1Corinthians 14:40;
Colossians 1:16–17; Proverbs 16:9; Jeremiah 10:23

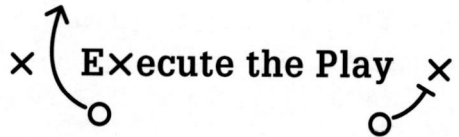

## Execute the Play

Plan for success. Have a plan for each tomorrow. Begin by praying. Ask God to direct you to what He wants you to accomplish. Weed out the distractions and distracters. Gather the tools you will need in order to be successful. Now, get busy.

# A Picture of Praise

n Pittsburg, they call them the Terrible Towels. Almost every NFL team has them. You know, a hand towel with the team logo imprinted on it. On January 22, 2006, during the NFC championship game, the Seattle fans came out in droves. And when they waved their towels, the image was nothing short of impressive. Almost every fan was waving a team towel. And their cheering was deafening.

The Seahawks carried the game to a decisive win: 34–14. The fans nearly propelled the stadium to greater heights as they twirled those team towels. Though Troy and Joe were in the broadcaster's booth, there was no need for commentary. That snapshot in the stadium was worth a thousand words and more. It was a picture of praise.

Walk into a Christian concert or consecrated church worship service and you will see a similar sight: a large group of people gathered together, hands and hearts lifted high, uninhibited cheering and adoration of our holy God. The victory has been won and jubilation cannot be restrained. The outpouring of the people's joy can't be contained. It is a picture of praise.

Many people think that praise is something we do for God. But I'd like to challenge that concept a bit. The Bible tells us that God inhabits the praise of His people. Let me list some of the benefits of praise. There is power and freedom in praise. Think about it. We're reviewing the qualities, attributes, and past victories of God in order to proclaim them. As we do this, the act of praising God renews our faith and restores a sense of hope. Both of these are depression-busters. In addition, as we sing or shout, we are stimulating the flow of oxygen to our lungs, hearts, and brains. This increased flow of oxygen gives us more physical, emotional, and spiritual energy. Perhaps the most significant contribution to our health is how praise reminds us that we're part of the winning team. It is impossible to feel defeated when the truth disputes those lies of inadequacy and failure.

When God takes a snapshot of us, let's make sure He sees a picture of praise

"But thou art holy, O thou that inhabitest the praises of Israel" (Psalm 22:3, KJV).

## Study the Playbook

READ: Psalm 103:2; Psalm 28:6; Psalm 66:20

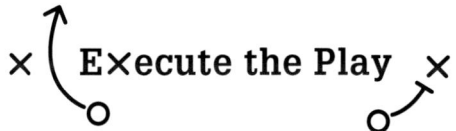

## Execute the Play

Every day, think of (at least) five good things God has done or is doing for you. Write a thank you note to Him. It doesn't matter whether you use paper, your smart phone, or your computer. What is important is that you do it! Finish it up by reading your thank you note out loud to God.

_____

_____

_____

_____

_____

_____

_____

_____

_____

_____

_____

_____

_____

# Champ or Chump?

C hamp. Chump. Only change one letter, but the definition is a life of immeasurable difference. The champion is a conqueror while the chump is conquered. How can a man become the conquering champion?

Emmitt Smith, Roger Staubach, Reggie White, Troy Aikman, Jerry Rice, John Elway, Bubba Smith, Randy White, Mike Singletary—these game greats share something in common: they each had a coach who modeled and required excellence.

Though a woman shoulders the incredible responsibility of birthing a son, she cannot give him the call he is created to answer. It takes a man to call a boy into manhood. Why is it so difficult to find men who are willing to mentor boys and younger men in the faith? God commanded it. The early church leaders modeled it. But today, in our politically correct society, we have pews full of men who don't. Perhaps these men are afraid of offending others. Or maybe they just don't want to pay the price of getting involved. Whatever the excuse, I can guarantee you that it won't fly with God. Our head coach is not one who cares to have His calls challenged or ignored.

Are you a young man (or young in the faith)? If so, you need a coach (mentor) to lead you into success. Your assignment: ask your church leaders to put you on a champion's team.

Are you a mature man (both in years and faith)? Then God has chosen you to join His team of assistant coaches. There are many who are counting on you to get off the bench and get in the game. Your job: ask your coach (pastor) how he can best use you to help the team (church) win.

Champ or chump: the only difference is *u*.

Teach the older men to be temperate, worthy of respect, self-controlled, and sound in faith, in love and in endurance ... encourage the young men to be self-controlled. In everything set them an example by doing what is good. In your teaching show integrity, seriousness and soundness of speech that cannot be condemned, so that those who oppose you may be ashamed because they have nothing bad to say about us.

Titus 2:2, 6–8

# Study the Playbook

**READ:** Hebrews 12:5–11;
1 Chronicles 29:17; Proverbs 3:11–12; 2 Timothy 2:15

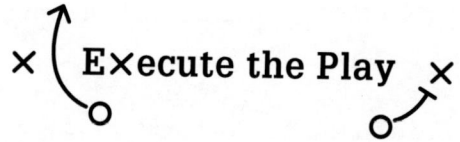

## Execute the Play

You need a coach. Find a mature Christian. Ask him to meet with you on a regularly, scheduled time. (Maybe once a week, over coffee. It doesn't matter where or when. It only matters that you do it.) Study. Learn. Apply.

# Forgiven and Forgotten

O n September 24, 2000, Terrell Owens committed an unpardonable sin in the sight of most Cowboys fans. After scoring a touchdown, he ran out to mid-field to the infamous logo, lifted his arms in victory and stood on the lone star. He was making a statement: he had conquered the star. That might not sound too offensive to you, but to the thousands of fans watching, his arrogant stance was one of dis-respect and disdain. The fans went wild with outrage. The game was not through. Emmitt Smith answered with a touchdown of his own. But his demeanor was totally different. His was that of humility and honor as he knelt down on the star. The stadium roared with cheers of approval. Frustration returned to Texas Stadium when T.O. scored another touchdown. Undaunted (and apparently hardheaded), Terrell just had to give an encore performance of his theatrics on the star. This time, however, justice (in the form of George Teague) was waiting for him. He met T.O. at the star with a hit that sent stars flashing before Ter-

rell's eyes. The stands went wild. For most Dallas fans, the final score was obscured as their memory stopped with the hammer of justice coming down.

In the years since this fateful day, T.O. has kept the press hot with a slew of wild antics both on and off the field. His behavior has earned him a reputation that has preceded him everywhere he's gone. His former team gave him numerous chances to change his ways. Finally, T.O. broke the last straw. He was benched for the rest of the season and then released. Speculation was rampant. Commentators and fans wondered which team in their right mind would be willing to consider taking on T.O. There was some doubt as to whether he was marketable at all. There were those few who seemed fearless (or crazy) enough to entertain the thought of bringing T.O. to their team. To the dismay of most Cowboys fans, Jerry Jones was the man who was willing to take on that risk. A shrewd businessman, Mr. Jones made certain the contract was packed with carefully laid-out boundaries and consequences for any unwanted behavior from this newest team member.

T.O. was the man who had disgraced the star. And now he was going to wear the star. When he came out onto the field, he was met with cheers and jeers. For many fans, that fateful day of dissing the star has not been forgotten, much less forgiven. To some, he had committed an 'unpardonable sin'.

Have you committed what you believe to be an unpardonable sin? Do you see your crimes against the cross so hideous that you don't know how you can ever wear one again? Do you think yourself too hideous to come before God? King David was such a man, burdened with the weight of sin and guilt. Jealousy, covetousness, lust, adultery, murder, and lying were his chief sins. He too wondered how he could ever come before the God he had so disregarded with his sinful acts. But as he sought after God, our loving Father revealed His character to David. This revelation was passed down to us all when David said, "He has taken our sins away from us as far as the east is from the west" (Psalm 103:12, NCV).

This verse gives us cause for great rejoicing and peace. Although fans might not forgive and forget, our Father does. Friend, our Father has forgiven and forgotten your sins. That's worth a star and more.

## Study the Playbook

**READ:** 1 John 1:9, 2:1; Acts 3:19; Isaiah 43:25

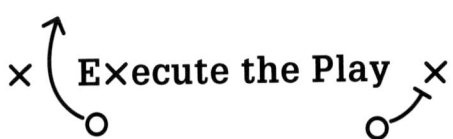

## Execute the Play

When you begin to replay your past failures, stop. Have you confessed these wrongs to the Lord? And have you turned away from repeating those sins? If you have, it's time to move on in His grace and forgiveness. Quote aloud these verses. Remind yourself that God has forgiven you. That's enough.

# How Can We Compare?

On December 27, 2005, Coach Tony Dungy and his wife, Lauren, had to do something no parent wants to do. They buried their eighteen-year-old son, James. What a crushing load of grief. How could this be? Coach Dungy and his Indianapolis Colts were in the last chapters of a Cinderella season. James was an excellent student and a good son. The Dungys were living godly lives. They were the poster family for Christianity. Then the monster of suicide attacked. Would they, *could* they continue to live for Christ?

Perhaps it's easier to answer these questions with another question or two. How can we compare the cruelty of our enemy with the goodness of our God? And how can we compare the cold and emptiness of this world with the faithfulness of our Father? Under the siege of grief ravaged thoughts, one must break away and ponder this question. How can we compare the yesterdays we've experienced to the tomorrows we've yet to know? To judge God by the thoughts or actions of this world, the enemy or ourselves makes for a dangerous mindset. During that dance, there comes a point of no return.

Yet, too many Christians fall into that trap. We think of God as a cosmic Santa Claus. When He gives us all that we could possibly dream of and performs miracles in opening doors of great opportunities, we say He is good. We justify this mentality by saying that He's fulfilling His promises to provide an abundant life. It might sound and feel good, but rationalizing doesn't make it right. While it is true that God promises to bless His children, He never promises to shield us from all trials and heartaches.

Job was a man who lived a godly life. Perhaps you remember the story of his life. A wealthy, influential man with a large family, it seemed that God delighted in pouring out blessings on Job. Apparently, Job lived in such a manner that it drew the attention of our arch enemy. Satan came before God to see what could be done to destroy the life and testimony of this man, Job. (Please note that this vile enemy had to ask God's permission.) After their discussion, God allowed a time of testing. What ensued was crushing for Job. He lost almost everything: his wealth, his ten children, his employees, and his health. This man had every human reason to turn his back on God. But even in his darkest hour, Job held onto his faith. He answered doubt (and doubters) by saying, "Though He slay me, yet will I trust him" (Job 13:15, NKJV).

You might be going through some hard times. The Dungy family sure has. While it would be easy to dismiss or disregard God, let me encourage you, just as the Dungy family has, to hold strong to His love. There is no other love that can compare.

> "Greater love has no one than this, that he lay down his life for his friends" (John 15:13).

## Study the Playbook

**READ:** Psalm 34:7–9, 18;
Philippians 4:6–7; Lamentations 3:22–23

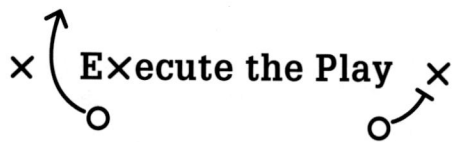

## Execute the Play

When you experience a loss, review these and other verses of God's eternal love and comfort. Copy and post them where you can see them everyday. Say and pray them out loud. His peace will come.

# One Last Tick

**D**umbfounded and numb, we sat and stared at the scoreboard.

It had been a grueling game, one that had been hammered out on every down. The lead had changed from our opponent to us and back more times than our wearied minds could recall. After a strong rally, we had a solid score. Momentum was on our side, or so it seemed. And then they drove down the field. Like a really bad dream, our defense could only muster slow-motion attempts against a rapid onslaught from their offense. We watched as they scored against our battle-worn defenders.

Yet there was a glimmer of hope. Less than a minute left-but if we put it all out on the field we just might get our kicker down into field goal range. Our offense took the field. Hearts raced with a strong tonic of urgency, laced with sheer panic and a splash of hope. A bullet of a pass, and our wide-out dove for the sidelines. The fans were almost rabid with anticipation. Hope was beginning to grow. Did we dare? But we had to! It was the only way to stretch for victory. Another pass-almost intercepted-fell incomplete. Third down and just a sprinkle of seconds left. A hand-off to the running back only netted a few yards, but it did get us to the center hash. Quickly, timeout was called. Six seconds left. Our kicking unit came onto the field. The mark was at the distant edge of our kicker's range. Yet, a successful boot would be enough to put us in the win column. The ball was snapped, set, and our kicker cut loose with enough torque that could have driven that ball to Mars. On the way to victory, the ball took a strange turn. *Doink!* The football slammed into the goalpost and crashed down left of the goal. We stood and watched as the last tick of the clock took us to the game-ending buzzer and defeat. Stunned and numb, we could only sit and stare at the scoreboard, dizzy. Our world began to spin. There was a sick feeling in the pit of every stomach. Unanswered questions echoed in the halls of our minds.

We tried to hush all the noise outside of the hospital room. ICU, an austere room filled with monitors, charts, and mysteriously ominous equipment. Tubes and wires were attached in every possible fashion. She was stable but critical. Although she had taken a lot of hits, almost miraculously, she began to rally. Whispers of hope hinted that she might get to go home on the weekend. After all, she had the best that Western medicine could offer: multimillion dollars worth of equipment, advanced medication, brilliantly trained and experienced medical personnel. In the midst of our growing hope, suddenly, another heart attack ripped at her frail body. In spite of the best man had to offer, her heart beat its last and she whispered her final breath. A flat line declared that our loved one had lost the battle. Stunned, with a sick feeling in the pit of our stomachs, we stared at the still monitors as the silence of the room began to scream out our pain.

A gridiron loss. The death of a precious loved one. Hopelessly final. Or is it? Death is *not* the final word. Paul encouraged us all when he said, "'Death has been swallowed up in victory'... thanks be to God! He gives us the victory through our Lord Jesus Christ" (1 Corinthians 15:54, 57)

For the Christian, hope is the pavement that our dearly departed walks on through the door of death into a glorious home in eternity. Though we miss this loved one, we can cling to the hope of eternal life in Christ Jesus, the final victory.

## Study the Playbook

**READ:** Psalm 30:5, 73:26; Isaiah 25:8; Nahum 1:7

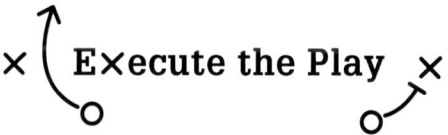

## Execute the Play

Grieving the loss of a loved one brings very real pain. Give yourself permission to take the full amount of time necessary to go through this journey. Join the Grief Share program at your church. Don't walk this path alone.

Written in loving memory of my mother, Mrs. Eva C. Bassett, who went to be with our Lord Jesus on August 25, 2006.

# Instant Replay

**W**as it a touchdown? No signal yet. Everyone is waiting for the field judge to give his ruling. Finally, he gives the signal for touchdown. Now comes the opposing coach's red flag. Yes, he has challenged the ruling on the field. The head referee announces the challenge and there's an official time out while he goes under the hood. After what seems an eternity (a minute and a half), he comes back with his ruling. This time, there is sufficient evidence to overturn the ruling on the field. The wide receiver had stepped out of bounds at the one-yard line. The six points have been erased, and it's a different ball game. Funny what this instant replay can do. A missed assignment, a poor tackle, a bad read all atoned for in the clean sweep of the overturned call. How much of football history has been altered, thanks to this slice of technology we call 'instant replay'?

Just imagine what it would be like if God gave us the power to go under the hood. How many moments, decisions, and actions would you like to have back? Some might wish to take back years lost to drug addiction. Others pray they could erase the devastation pornography and moral impurity brought on their family. Maybe your heart aches to turn back the clock and bring back to life the baby you aborted. The list of regrets goes on and on, as does the endless longing to turn back time and somehow get back what was lost.

Is there a spiritual instant replay? Well, yes and no. Let me explain. We learn that "anyone united with the Messiah gets a fresh start, is created new. The old life is gone" (2 Corinthians 5:17, MSG).

Spiritually, there is an ocean full of second chances. God forgives and cleanses (1 John 1:9). But there is also the reality of temporal consequences. There might be legal ramifications or fines to pay. Even though God is in the healing business, there might be some hearts and relationships so broken that they refuse to be mended. Yet, God's grace is sufficient to sustain us to the end (2 Corinthians 12:9). No, there is no instant replay in life that erases our *mistakes*; but there is a loving Savior who takes away our *sins*. And that's a call that won't ever be overturned!

## Study the Playbook

READ: 2 Corinthians 9:8; 1 Peter 5:10; Titus 3:7

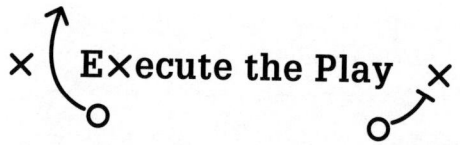

## Execute the Play

It's time to pick up the pieces. Obedience is one of the best balms to speed healing. Choose a book in the Bible and delve into studying God's Word. Pick up your heart's phone and talk to Him. And while you're on this journey of growth and healing, don't be afraid to seek out a Christian counselor for support and help.

_____

_____

_____

_____

_____

_____

_____

_____

_____

_____

_____

# Looking On

**D**efeated. The game of the year is over. Everything you've trained for; you did your best, but it wasn't enough. Crushed, you feel lost in a sea of faces. It all seems so surreal. Just a few brief hours ago, the world clamored for even a glimpse of you. Not now. Fickle loyalty; allegiance now spells abandonment. No one wants anything to do with a loser. The security detail shoves you aside. Numb, you're left looking on as the winners are ushered into victory's celebration. As they hoist up the trophy, it rains colored confetti, their colors. Head hung, bitter tears pour out of your broken heart. Accolades and stats don't matter. You came so close, but...

Everything you've worked and lived for lies in shattered pieces. You've done your best, but it wasn't enough. You feel crushed and lost. Just a few brief moments ago, the world clamored after you, promising everything your heart could desire. That was then. But now you're shoved aside and abandoned, you look on as the victors are ushered in. Burning fire rains down as you watch the gates fade into an infinite distance. Accolades and affluence, acquisitions and accomplishments—none of that matters now (Ephesians 2:8–9). You came so close, but...

For the team who lost this year's Super Bowl, there is always next year's big game. But for the deceased, there are no more tomorrows, no more chances.

"Man is destined to die once, and after that to face judgment" (Hebrews 9:27).

An eternity of looking on into the heavenly bliss that could have been, a tormenting glimpse of the beginning of an eternity separated from God; could this be your reality? It doesn't have to be. Thankfully, God has made a way for you to avoid disaster and enter into heaven through His gates.

"The gift of God is eternal life in Christ Jesus our Lord" (Romans 6:23b).

Triumph or torment? The choice is yours. Won't you choose Christ?

## Study the Playbook

**READ**: Isaiah 59:2; Romans 5:8; 1 John 5:11–12

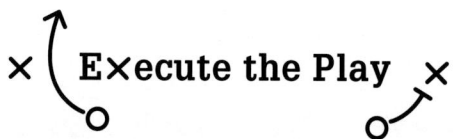

## Execute the Play

If you've never booked your passage to Heaven, it's time to take care of that, now! Admit that you aren't perfect and are unqualified to enter into Heaven. Acknowledge that you do need a perfect Savior. Receive His gift of eternal life. Now turn away from all forms of rebellion and choose to honor God with all you say, think and do.

# Meeting the Media

Check out the recent sports news. The media has been swarming around another young player. The big scoop is about his lack of wisdom in choosing his off-field entertainment. He made a mistake in judgment. Lots of details, but suffice it to say the bottom line is his choice of activity led to an accident. Now that he's injured, there are some doubts about his viability for this upcoming season.

You might wonder why he hasn't received more sympathy from the press, but rather why he has come under such great scrutiny. Perhaps it's because of the bundle of dough the team has coughed up to sign him. And now, because of his foolish and selfish decision, he will be on the bench. He has negatively impacted his career as well as the team's chances for victory while he's on the injured-reserved list.

You remember Jesus teaching His disciples the principle of responsibility. He told them that much is required of those to whom much is given. (Luke 12:48) God has given this athlete an incredible talent, and man (his team) has given him great wealth. Both man and God have the right to require commitment, excellence, and integrity from this young man.

We might think we're exempt from this kind of accountability. We have no media crews at our doors or multi-million-dollar contracts hanging over our heads. Yet, there are those in our workplace and home who depend on us to keep the promises we've committed to them. I doubt there will be any great meeting of the media for many of us. But we will all have a day of reckoning, a day we must account to God for what we've done with the gifts He's given to us. Instead of scorn, I want to hear God commend me. You too? Then let's commit to a lifestyle of integrity and covenant-keeping so that we may indeed hear those powerful and fulfilling words, "Well done, good and faithful servant" (Matthew 25:21a).

## Study the Playbook

**READ:** Luke 12:35–48;
Micah 6:8; Deuteronomy 10:12

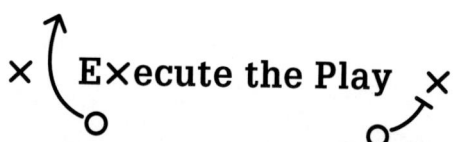

## Execute the Play

There is no solo act in football or the Christian life. Do more than just attend; get involved in your church. Find an area where your abilities match their needs. Become a part of a Bible study. Ask a trustworthy, mature Christian to be your prayer and accountability partner. Meet with him each week. Give him permission to speak honestly and directly about your life choices. Apply what you are taught.

# Put Your Money Where Your Mouth Is

Deion Sanders, fastest man in the NFL; "Prime Time"; flashiest, most flamboyant character of the NFL; "Neon Deion"; one of the wealthiest in the league; yet, he was so haunted by feelings of unworthiness that he was willing to take his life.

In 1997, he attempted suicide by driving his car over a cliff. His attempt was not sufficient to thwart God's plans. Miraculously, Deion walked away from the accident without a scratch. Following this near-tragedy he was approached by several godly men. They shared God's truths with him. Over a relatively short span of time Deion committed his life to Christ as his personal Savior.

God took this same Neon Deion. Yes, his heart had been changed toward Christ; but God had plans to use Deion's colorful personality. Deion was so thrilled to be free from the pain of emptiness that he wanted to tell the whole world what God had done for him. But the world wasn't very receptive. All the masses could see was "Prime Time." Deion soon learned that he would have to prove the genuineness of his faith, and that would be through Christ-like living and time.

Because he was "Neon Deion", the media stayed hot on his heels. No doubt they thought a fall from grace would make a great story. Instead, what they dug up was grace in action. Deion pursued obedience to Christ with the same intensity he would use to capture a sprinting receiver. He learned of God's command to tithe. Tithing is a 'God thing'. It doesn't make sense to the general public. As the media continued to dig for dirt, what they came upon was Deion's tithing record. You can imagine the media's confusion when they discovered the large sums of money Deion had tithed. "Prime Time" had put his money where his mouth was. His actions were backing up the story he had shared with the world. But Deion had learned that God is the ultimate Promise-Keeper.

> "Bring the full 10 percent into the storehouse so that there may be food in My house. Test me in this way," says the Lord of Hosts. "See if I will not open the floodgates of heaven and pour out a blessing for you without measure."
>
> Malachi 3:10 (HCSB)

God has honored Deion for his choices of obedience. Why not put God to the test and see what He will do for you?

# Study the Playbook

**READ:** Luke 6:38;
Proverbs 3:9–10; 2 Corinthians 9:7

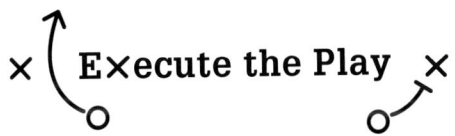

## Execute the Play

Look at the gross income on your paystub.
Open your checkbook and write out 10% of
that amount. At church, give it to God. Now,
wait and watch. You just freed God to bless
you!

# Spending Millions

We read and hear in the news about the multi-million-dollar contracts that are awarded to promising athletes. Some people complain about the large sums of money given to just one person. Perhaps those complaining don't realize that all money comes with its own price tag. Jesus gave a timeless principle when He said, "From everyone who has been given much, much will be demanded; and from the one who has been entrusted with much, much more will be asked" (Luke 12:48b).

The world of sports expects the athlete to perform to almost superhero standards. And society in general scrutinizes how those superstar athletes spend their millions. Often, we learn of athletes squandering thousands of dollars on wild parties and other illicit behaviors. In contrast, it is comforting to know how generous the NFL and many of its athletes are with their fortunes. Approximately two hundred NFL players have established foundations to help benefit those in their community. And the NFL, through its charities, awards $1,000,000 in grants per year to support

the philanthropic work of current and former players. After the tragedy of 9/11, the league responded by
establishing a $10 million NFL Disaster Relief Fund.

Why is it that so many think they have the higher
moral ground from which to judge another person's
use of his earnings? Isn't that a rather dangerous ledge
on which to stand? Jesus encountered religious sects
who struggled with self-righteousness. He warned
them, "Do not judge, or you too will be judged. For
in the same way you judge others, you will be judged,
and with the measure you use, it will be measured to
you" (Matthew 7:1–2).

Someone could be watching us and scrutinizing
our financial decisions. We too could be interrogated
with such questions as, "Do you have any personal
debt?" "Do you pay your tithe?" "Do you pay your bills
on time?" Jesus might respond as He did to the critics
of His day with a question of His own:

> Why do you look at the speck of sawdust in your
> brother's eye and pay no attention to the plank in
> your own eye? How can you say to your brother,
> "Let me take the speck out of your eye," when all
> the time there is a plank in your own eye?
>
> Matthew 7:3–4

I'm certainly not suggesting that everyone in the
game is innocent or handles their finances well. That
would be naive and ignorant. Rather, the spiritual lesson is that we should be less critical of others and
exercise greater personal responsibility and discipline.
Should God want to entrust me to the management
of millions of dollars, I want to make sure I've demonstrated decisions worthy of such trust. Wouldn't you?

# Study the Playbook

**READ:** Proverbs 21:5; Proverbs 25:28;
Haggai 2:8; Proverbs 13:22

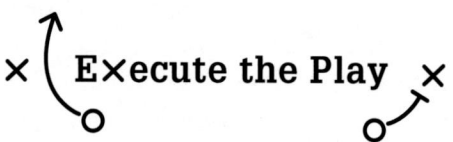

## Execute the Play

The economy is never a sure thing. Be wise and look after your family. Honor God with your money management. Tithe on every paycheck. Save for emergencies and retirement. Create a budget and live within those boundaries. Pay your bills on time.

_____

_____

_____

_____

_____

_____

_____

_____

_____

_____

# Ten to Tragedy, Two to Triumph

**E**very team wants to end up in gridiron's promised land: the Super Bowl. You would think that owners and coaches would do everything within their power to make wise decisions in building their team for success. But just look around the league. Count all the teams that have built their team around one or two talented players. It makes one wonder, what they were thinking when they stacked their odds of winning so steeply on just a small few. Did they really believe that one or two could stand up against eleven (or, twenty-two)? Did they do their math? It doesn't add up too well in my math books, and game day scores are proof that they keep coming up short.

It's ironic how great intentions and poor decisions go hand in hand. History serves up a good example. God told Moses to select some men to check out the Promised Land (Canaan) He was giving to them. Talk about an incredible real estate deal. They were to investigate, come back, and report. Then they were to go and acquire what God had promised them. Sounds great? It was supposed to be. Twelve great leaders, one representing each tribe of Israel, went out on this stealth mission. They discovered that the land was as sweet of a deal as God had told them it would be. But they also came across an obstacle that seemed too great for them: gigantic warriors. Ten of those scouts advised the nation to turn and run. Two (Joshua and Caleb) stood on God's promises and urged their nation to trust God and take Canaan by storm. Sadly, the Israelites followed the ten to tragedy. Not only did their decision cost them the land but their lives as well. They died as wanderers in the desert. The next generation followed the two to triumph. Joshua and Caleb took God at His Word and led their people into the Promised Land.

All of us face challenges. Too many of us hope and wish for good things to come our way. But good intentions only produce empty pockets and broken dreams. If we are ever going to enjoy God's promises, we must begin by studying His plans for us (found in the Bible). And just as Joshua and Caleb did, we must trust God at His Word. Finally, we must put into action all that He directs us to do. Then we can count on God to lead us to triumph over any foe and into the successes He has planned for us.

> Joshua son of Nun and Caleb son of Jephunneh, who were among those who had explored the land, tore their clothes and said to the entire Israelite assembly, "The land we passed through and explored is exceedingly good. If the LORD is pleased with us, he will lead us into that land, a land flowing with milk

and honey, and will give it to us. Only do not rebel against the Lord. And do not be afraid of the people of the land, because we will swallow them up. Their protection is gone, but the LORD is with us. Do not be afraid of them.

Numbers 14: 6–9

## Study the Playbook

**READ:** Jeremiah 29:11–13; Psalm 37:23; Proverbs 16:9; Proverbs 3:5–6

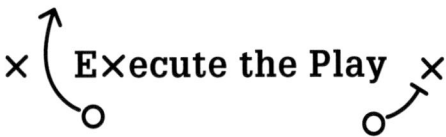

God gave Joshua and Caleb a dream, and He has given you one as well. Stop wishing it will come true. Write down your dream. Write down achievable goals that will help you accomplish this dream. Ask for wise counsel from people in the field. Work hard. Be wise. And never give up!

_____

_____

_____

_____

_____

# The Crushing Weight

**H**eavy-handed. "That's a five-hundred-dollar fine." Tough-minded. "Do it again. We'll stay out here all day until you get it right." A cutting tongue. "What are you doing? You're killing me." A task-master. "Give me fifty. When you're through, bring me some water. And be quick about it." By now, you've probably guessed I'm describing the typical head coach. Relentless and seemingly heartless, he pushes and presses his players to stretch for excellence. He's striving to get the best out of each man for the greater good of the team. Come game day, he's a different man. Encouraging and inspiring, he sends his players onto the field with a sense of empowerment. After a series well-executed, the athlete beams under the pats and "atta-boys" from his coach. The rough handling during those tough practices has paid off in a victory for the day.

Now rewind that scene to a different playback. There is no letup from the barrage of put-downs. Criticism, judgment, and harshness are a regular

diet dished out. Give it all you've got, yet it's never enough—no praise, no victory. Under that type of training, the scoreboard would probably reveal a loss for the day. But even worse, there would be a locker room full of disheartened and defeated men.

Coaches aren't the only ones capable of destroying those under their tutelage. A poor grade followed by a teacher's cruel words of degradation can be paralyzing to that teenager striving for academic success. A business setback accompanied by a boss' sarcastic words of disgust can haunt the adult still hungering for the approval of a father. A moral failure trailed by slashing words of judgment from a spiritual leader can shatter an already-broken church member. Tragically, all are doomed to crumble under the crushing weight of condemnation.

Where does this spirit of judgment and condemnation come from? Legalism. It's a system and mindset of living by and under the law. Ironically, it was God who designed the law to show our inability to reach perfection and heaven.

"So the good law, which was supposed to show me the way of life, instead gave me the death penalty" (Romans 7:10, NLT).

Then how is it that there are those who still insist on living in this prison of legalism? It was one of the major issues which earned the wrath of our Lord Jesus. When he met leaders wielding legalism He confronted them.

"You hypocrite, first take the plank out of your own eye, and then you will see clearly to remove the speck from your brother's eye" (Matthew 7:5).

So what is our solution for today? How are we to combat these legalistic attacks? Paul taught us to remember that, "there is now no condemnation for those who are in Christ Jesus" (Romans 8:1).

Friend, crawl out from under that boulder of blame. No more crushing weight! You've been set free (John 8:36).

## Study the Playbook

**READ:** 1 Corinthians 6:20; 1 John 3:1–2; John 15:15; Romans 6:18; Proverbs 18:21

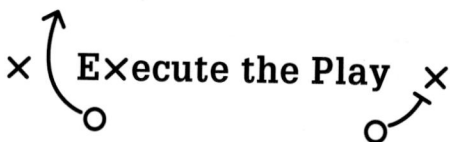

## Execute the Play

Know what God says about you. Read these verses out loud. Repeat them until they are engraved in your mind. When others judge and criticize you, remind yourself what God thinks of you.

# Two-minute Warning

The game's been exciting and tight. Through four quarters, the coaches have played an intense game of chess. It's now down to the wire. The officials give the infamous two-minute warning, and the teams get a much-needed break to the sidelines. In this frantic timeout the coaches strategize and remind the team of the plays they've prepared throughout the week. The officials whistle to announce that the timeout is complete. The players take the field. These are the deciding moments. Soon one team will rejoice in victory while the other will slip away in the solemnity of loss.

It's an interesting animal, this two-minute warning. Much of what transpires is a combination of two unlikely bedfellows. There is the intense strategizing partnered with the calm of operating on autopilot. The players, if coached well, begin to execute the game plan without having to think about their next step. There's a reason why. Throughout the week, they have studied the game book. They have practiced the plays they need to execute. They have run through seemingly endless two-minute drills. In a word, they are prepared.

Does your life ever feel like you're in the middle of a two-minute warning? There's no pressure quite like those last few moments before you punch in at work, just barely beating the clock; those last minute reports that must be submitted to the board; or the last moments before they close the gate to the last flight out for the day. Under these torqued conditions, what is squeezed out of you? Jesus gives us an interesting insight:

> "But the things that come out of the mouth come from the heart, and these make a man 'unclean'" (Matthew 15:18).

What's on the inside will be reflected in your speech (Matthew 15:10–20).

Like the coach trains his team to execute the two-minute drill, Peter coached all believers to be prepared with this solid game plan on how to live a victorious life:

- Have an attitude of unity
- Be compassionate
- Be loving
- Be tenderhearted
- Be courteous
- Don't be vengeful
- Bless others
- Share Christ with everyone.

1 Peter 3:8–15

How's your two-minute drill? Ready to live the victorious Christian life?

## Study the Playbook

**READ:** Ephesians 4:25–32;
Proverbs 15:1; Philippians 2:14–15

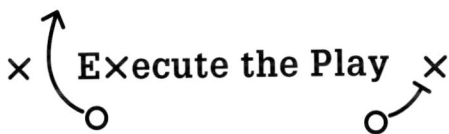

Study the Christian's two minute drill. Read, learn and apply these Scripture verses. Become a living Bible for all to read.

_____

_____

_____

_____

_____

_____

_____

_____

_____

_____

_____

# Used Up

Remember your first new car? I do. I showed it to every warm body I could drag out to see it. I loved that new car smell. I washed and waxed it. I made sure it had the best oil, gasoline, and regular maintenance. But somewhere between time and life, the car developed a problem: mileage, and a lot of it. The newness had long worn off. Soon, it began making lots of weird sounds. Repair bills began to add up. It didn't take long for me to realize that it was becoming a liability to own. It was no longer cost-effective for me to own it. The decision was just business. There was a man who was willing to take it off my hands and put a bit of cash in them as well. And that was that.

Remember when you signed your contract? At the press conference, you held up your new jersey. Your coach and GM were beaming over you. The only thing shining brighter was the smile on your face. Throughout the first season, the press, coaches, and fans had only praise and admiration to give. But somewhere between time and life, a problem developed: mileage, and a lot of it; an ache here and a pain there. Injuries began to add up. From their point of view, you were used up. It didn't take long for them to realize it was becoming a liability to have you on the roster. The decision was just business. You were released. They were ready to move on, but you were left to live with the stench of their rejection.

We're a society that consumes people and relationships with the same speed and nonchalance as we do our fast-food dinners. Whether on the gridiron, the business world, high school halls, or in the family, you've seen these stories played out, maybe in your own life. Our hearts cry out to know if there is anyone who really cares. Turn to the Old Testament and look at Job. Life and his friends had used him up and hung him out to dry. But God didn't. Job asked, "What is man, that you think so highly of him and pay so much attention to him?" (Job 7:17, HCSB).

God doesn't think you're used up. He still has a game plan for you (Jeremiah 29:11). What are you waiting for? Take the field (of life) and finish strong (1 Corinthians 9:24).

## Study the Playbook

READ: John 15:16;
Ephesians 2:10; Philippians 1:6, 4:13

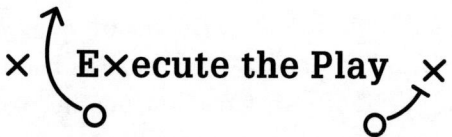

## Execute the Play

Tune out what the worlds says. Concentrate only on what God says about you. Read these verses about His love for and value of you. Seek out more verses that affirm your value. Recite them until they become a permanent part of your thinking.

_____

_____

_____

_____

_____

_____

_____

_____

_____

_____

_____

_____

_____

_____

# The O-line

The offensive line is a group of men crucial to the success of a winning drive. Center, tackles, and guards come together to perform two major tasks: open up holes for the running backs and, no matter what, protect their quarterback. Though their efforts are essential for the team to experience success, the media and fans rarely notice, much less appreciate, them. Yet most of these men are driven by the silent satisfaction of knowing they have done their job and done it well.

Think of your favorite quarterback. Can you imagine sending one of the greats into a game to stand behind just a center? What kind of coach would send in his top quarterback without the full protection of the offensive line? What a nightmare! There is no way the team could mount any offensive effort. The quarterback would always be sacked. No matter how elite, savvy, or swift he might be, the defense would be sending in their linebacker core for an all-you-can-eat QB buffet. It's an absurd picture-one that will never take place on any football field.

For a moment, let's turn our gaze to the Christian in a local church. We are the QB in our personal lives. Jesus, our head coach, is responsible for calling in the right plays to help us achieve victory. Now let's take a look at just a few of the opponents we must face: lust, seduction, envy, jealousy, sorrow, depression, fear, procrastination, gossip, criticalness, rage, hatred, temptation, and addiction. In order for us to be successful, we must have a spiritual O-line. Though not every O-line looks the same, some of these key teammates are our pastors, associate ministers, Bible study teachers and members, specific support groups, prayer partners, and mentors. Can you imagine our head coach, Jesus, sending us into the game of life without an effective O-line? It will never happen. This is one of the reasons He created the church. Without the support of fellow believers, we will not experience the victory that Christ has claimed for us. Paul warned all Christians (past and present), that we "should not stay away from church meetings, as some are doing," but that we "should meet together and encourage each other" (Hebrews 10:25, NCV).

In our times of greatest need as well as our everyday challenges, we can thank God for His church, our powerful O-line, which helps speed us to victory in our Lord Jesus.

## Study the Playbook

**READ:** Romans 12:5;
1 Corinthians 12:12–27; Ecclesiastes 4:9–12

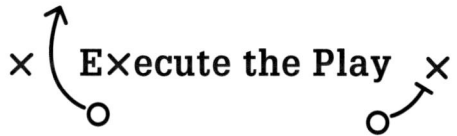

## Execute the Play

If you don't have a church home, begin your search for one this week. Keep looking until you find one that is a good fit for you and your family. If you're already a member of a church, be faithful to attend each week. Get connected with a home group and/or small Bible study.

_____

_____

_____

_____

_____

_____

_____

_____

_____

_____

_____

_____

# What's in a Name?

Too Tall, Hollywood, Minister of Defense, The Freak, The Bus, Big Ben, Rocket, The Refrigerator, Sweetness, The Snake, Prime Time: you recognize these nicknames of NFL greats, past and present. Some describe the size of the man or the way he played the game. Other nicknames capture the character of the man on and off the field.

What *is* in a name? The Bible says, "A good name is more desirable than great riches; to be esteemed is better than silver or gold" (Proverbs 22:1).

We've all watched expecting parents laboring over the choice of name for their firstborn child. Picking just the right name is so crucial. Many parents want their children to grow into and live up to that name.

Think about our nicknames. Sometimes, it's just the abbreviation of a longer name. Usually people tag us with one that describes something about us, such as a comment about our appearance. More often, though, a nickname describes the way we live, much like a quick advertisement to our character, our reputation in a capsule.

The Scriptures have something to say about this too. King David explained to his son that, "even a child is known by his actions, by whether his conduct is pure and right" (Proverbs 20:11). This teaching is still true for adults.

So what's in a name? Honor or shame, we create the billboard it will post for the world to see. Make yours a great one!

## Study the Playbook

**READ:** Philippians 2:4–7;
1 Thessalonians 5:22; 1 Corinthians 10:31

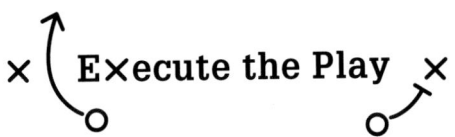

In all that you say, think and do, glorify God. Speak with honesty and kindness. Keep your thoughts pure and honorable. Accomplish, to a standard of excellence, all the tasks for which you are responsible.

(The names to match the above NFL greats: Ed Jones, Thomas Henderson, Reggie White, Javon Kearse, Jerome Bettis, Ben Roethlisberger, Raghib Ishmael, William Perry, Walter Payton, Jake Plummer and Ken Stabler, Deion Sanders.)

# When Dad Hung Up

t's draft weekend. There's a whirlwind of speculation as to who will be chosen in the first round. All the eligible athletes wait to hear their names called. Some wait in the special facilities set up by the NFL. Others wait at home with family and friends. Hopes and dreams hinge on a fateful phone call.

That's just how it was some years ago for my friend. Having been life-long fans of the local team, Harry* and his family were hoping for a call from the team's general manager. Sitting in the family living room, the family watched the TV coverage and waited. And then the phone rang. Harry's dad answered the phone. The caller identified himself as the owner and GM of a despised division rival. That was all Harry's dad needed to hear. In clear terms, he told this powerful GM that his boy was not interested in playing for the rival team. There would be no traitors in his house. Then he hung up the phone.

What was he doing? Harry's hopes hung on that call-didn't his dad know that? Apparently his family's loyalty to the home team took precedence over Harry's success. Stunned, Harry saw his dad choose fandom over family. While Harry was still pleading his case with his father, the baffled rival GM was bold enough to call back. Despite family tension, Harry was drafted.

God made Harry elusive and fast. He was masterfully designed to play the game. Harry's not the only one who is blessed. You also have a special gift from God. God has given you a special dream as well. Whether it's the NFL, motherhood, speaking to a packed hall, or winning an election, be careful. There will be those eager to attack your dream. They will criticize you, your giftedness, and your ability. Worst of all, they will doubt the God factor in your call. Think the ache you feel is a solo only your heart cries? Think again. Jesus was (and still is) the living Son of the Almighty God. Yet, the very people He should have been able to count on (family and community) turned on Him. They challenged Him.

> Where did this Man get this wisdom and this power to do miracles? He is just the son of a carpenter ... But Jesus said to them, "A prophet is honored everywhere except in his hometown and in his own home." So He did not do many miracles there because they had no faith.
>
> Matthew 13:54–58 (NCV)

Here's the game plan: surround yourself with those who celebrate you, your giftedness, and God's anointing in your life. After all, you have been drafted by the greatest GM ever: God our Master.

# Study the Playbook

**READ:** Isaiah 26:3, 54:17; Jeremiah 29:11;
Philippians 4:8; Proverbs 27:9, 17; Hebrews 10:24

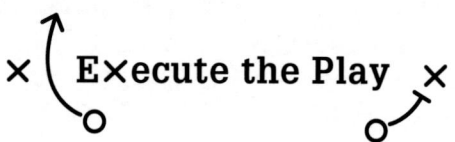

## Execute the Play

Look for people with a vision who are mature in their Christian faith. Get to know them. Spend time together on a regular basis. Listen to and encourage them in their pursuit of their dreams. Ask them to do the same for you. Pray together.

(*Name changed to protect the athlete's privacy.)

_____

_____

_____

_____

_____

_____

_____

_____

# A Tainted Victory

My team had suffered a surprising and humiliating loss. Along with thousands of other fans, players, and coaches, we were all eager to put that bad taste out of our mouths with the sweetness of a win. Playing against a bubble team from our conference, the game was important to us but crucial for our opponents. During the first half, the scoring was equally matched as momentum ebbed and flowed from both teams. It wasn't until the middle of the third quarter that my team began to pull away. In the fourth, we scored again and never looked back. Oh, the sweet aroma of victory! It swirled all around us. But then a rancid stench began to slip in to assail our nostrils. Soon, it permeated the locker room and every place where those satellite waves could bounce the news. One of our very own players had committed an unpardonable sin. He had spit in the face of an opposing player's face. Though he offered an apology, its effectiveness and his sincerity were immediately challenged. This despicable behavior did not go unnoticed by the league. They disciplined him with a $35,000

fine. Worse yet, many are saying that this player has lost the respect of all who play (or have played) in the NFL. At the day's end, it was a tainted victory.

This reminds me of a story in which scandalous behavior robbed an entire nation of the sweetness of a hard-fought victory. Turn back the pages of history to the reign of King David (2 Samuel 11–12). Right from the start, the setting was cast for disaster. For whatever reason, David chose to stay home instead of leading his men into battle. Things quickly begin to slip into a slimy pit of degradation. Was he bored and looking for some new excitement? It seems that he found it. His neighbor, Bathsheba, was a bathing beauty. David started off as a peeping Tom. But looking wasn't enough. His lust demanded that he have what he saw. Lust turned into passion as he sent for her and ordered her into his bed. What was yesterday's passion had become today's predicament: pregnancy. David tried to cover up his indiscretion by sending for Bathsheba's husband, Uriah. Obediently, he came home from the battle but refused to enjoy the comforts of home. He slept in the soldier's quarters instead. Since David couldn't trick Uriah into sleeping with his wife, David schemed to get rid of this man. David's plan was successful. Uriah was "killed in battle," freeing Bathsheba to come into David's house forever. Though the Israelites were victorious in battle, one couldn't miss the stench of adultery and murder. You know that God couldn't allow such debauchery to go unchecked. The death of this illegitimate son was just the beginning of *"Heartbreak Hotel" for David. It was another tainted victory.

Do you find yourself in a similar situation, trying to play the odds by continuing to lead a double life? Portraying a life of righteousness and success, you hide a secret sin. You too are living with a tainted victory. Don't be fooled: God isn't blind to your lies and schemes. Just as the league judged and disciplined this player and God judged and disciplined King David, you too will be called out to answer for your deeds. Before your scandal hits the news, you might better think about coming clean and making things right. For your sake and all those you love, I pray you do.

"Do not be deceived: God cannot be mocked. A man reaps what he sows" (Galatians 6:7).

## Study the Playbook

**READ:** Romans 12:21; 1 Corinthians 6:12–20, 10:13, 15:57; 2 Corinthians 2:14

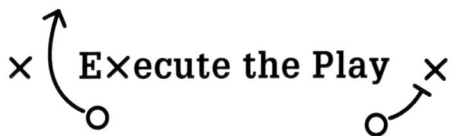

### Execute the Play

It's time to break old habits. Avoid people and places that have lured you into immoral activities. Break old cycles by getting involved in a support group. Make and develop new friends who live a Christ-like lifestyle.

*"Heartbreak Hotel" Lyrics by Tommy Durden, Music by Mae Axton and recorded by Elvis Presley

# Condemned
# in a Snap

He is the all-American, hometown boy stepping out of a Norman Rockwell picture. Growing up in a small, Wisconsin town, baby-faced, humble, and kind natured, it's not hard to see why many fans got caught up in Romo-mania. When he took over the QB helm, he had so much success at his start that it was almost magical. Much to the chagrin of Coach Parcells, most Cowboy fans were bringing out the oil in mid-November to anoint Tony Romo as Dallas's latest gridiron savior.

But then came December. The New Orleans Saints gave a couple of cold slaps to that baby face. Two more losses were dished out, but the Cowboys were still in the playoffs as a wild card. January 6, 2007 found the 'Boys' in Seattle facing the Seahawks and their Twelfth Man. Though both teams fought hard, it seemed that Parcells's boys were going to sit the Hawks on their home perch. With 1:19 remaining, the Cowboys lined up at the nineteen-yard line for what should be the winning field goal. As usual, Romo was the sure-handed holder. But then the nightmare began. The snap was good. Tony got his hands on the ball. But as he was turning the ball to set for the kick, somehow, it slipped through his fingers. As adrenaline surged through his body, he picked up the ball and began running for the end zone. Tackled at the one-and-a-half-yard line, his attempt proved futile. The game was lost, and the Cowboys' dash for the Lombardi was over.

After the game, cameras followed this broken boy into the locker room. Dejected, with his shoulders sunk and head down, Tony turned his back to the media in attempts to hide his gut-wrenching sorrow. No doubt images of what had just happened on the field were continuing to replay in his mind. During his post-game interview, Tony said that this mistake and game were going to be with him for a long time.

'Condemned' is defined as being declared unfit for use, disapproved of. While the condemnation we receive from others is often very painful, it is the condemnation we dish out to ourselves that is poisonous. Throughout life, we all experience some defeats. For some, like Tony (and the rest of his teammates), it's during a close game. But for most of us, it comes in the form of our daily challenges. Whether it is mismanaged resources, failed exams, disappointing quarterly results, lost opportunities, or relationships that have soured, all of us will face some defeats during our lifetime. The age-old question remains: how will we handle our failures? That you and I wrestle with this burden is nothing new. In ancient Rome, the early church struggled under the weight of condemnation. Paul sought to encourage and strengthen them in their faith when he said, "There is now no condemnation for those who are in Christ Jesus, because through Christ Jesus the law of the Spirit of life set me free" (Romans 8:1–2).

Child of God, shake off those shackles of condemnation and walk in the freedom of His love and grace.

## Study the Playbook

**READ:** Hebrews 4:14–16; Jude 1:24–25; Psalm 73:26

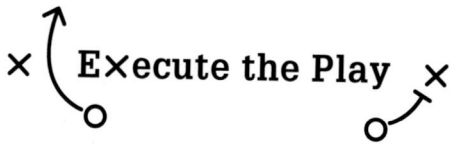

## Execute the Play

Just like King David did, you will have to learn to encourage yourself in the Lord. Read these and other reaffirming verses. Repeat them, out loud, every time you feel a wave of condemnation getting ready to wash over you.

_____

_____

_____

_____

_____

# Framed

It's enormous! Hanging ninety feet from the field, the thing stretches from one twenty-yard line to the other twenty-yard line. And it weighs in at a whopping eight hundred thousand pounds. Of course, I'm referring to the video board at the new Cowboys stadium in Arlington, Texas. Top this off with the sweetness that it's all in HD. The picture and the enormity of the board are incredible. You can see every little detail from any and every angle in the stadium. The coaches and fans won't miss a thing. What our eyes miss, the video board will catch.

As exciting as this is, there is a flip side. Whatever the camera sees, so does everyone else. Not so good news if a player is trying to get away with a jab to the ribs or a quick tug on the face mask. Though Jerry Jones was trying to create a Texas-sized statement, inadvertently he might have created a conscience for those on the field (and in the stands). Stated another way, people behave differently when they know they're being watched. But if a person thinks no one is watching, isn't it true that the real character comes shining through?

Let's take a peek on how this plays out in real life. You remember the man sitting next to you in church.

He had his game face on. But in the privacy of his home or office, he feels free to surf the Web for his favorite porn sites. And you saw that sweet mom at the PTA meeting. What you didn't see is that when the kids are off to school and her husband has left for work she heads out for that secret shopping spree they really can't afford.

It doesn't matter what the secret sin is. It's just that: secret. Rather it's the idea that it's secret. But is it truly secret? God says, "I see everything they do. They cannot hide from me the things they do; their sin is not hidden from my eyes" (Jeremiah 16:17, NCV).

Whether we realize it or not, God is watching. Don't get framed by your sin. But rather, live in honesty and integrity and your life will be picture perfect on the heavenly Father's mantle.

## Study the Playbook

**READ:** Psalm 69:5; James 4:17; Psalm 90:8

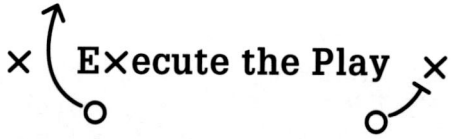

## Execute the Play

Stop pretending that you are able to sneak past God's sight. Be willing to get the support you need to break the chains of sinful behavior. Look up Christian counselors and support groups in your area. Be faithful to attend your sessions and apply all that you learn.

# How Much Did I Pay?

You love going to the game. Oh yeah. They say the best seat in town is in front of your television set. But there's nothing like being there personally, in the midst of all the action. The cameras can't capture the full experience. No. For it to be real to me, I need to experience it for myself.

Recently my family and I went to a game. We had great seats. It was an awesome game. But it really was shocking to see the prices. Each ticket had a hefty price tag. Now multiply that times four. Just to walk in the gates brought the price to a whopping total.

Here's how much we paid to walk in the gates: nothing, zero, zilch, nada. A friend of ours knew we wanted to go and that the cost was too much for us. The tickets were a gift. Without his gift, we couldn't have gone to the game.

Getting to go to the game reminds me a lot of getting to go to heaven. Know what it costs to get into heaven? Some think it's being good, committing random acts of kindness, and serving in the community

and church. These are all wonderful things to do. Only problem: they won't pass for a ticket when you get to the pearly gates. Here's the price of a ticket: live a perfect, sinless life, and withstand thirty-nine lashes, multiple beatings, a crown of thorns, crowds taunting and jeering, spitting, naked humiliation, three enormous nails, a spear thrust, and a broken heart. It's too much! There's no way you (or I) can pay that price. But there is good news. My Friend has paid for your ticket.

"God demonstrates His own love for us in this: While we were still sinners, Christ died for us" (Romans 5:8).

In fact, He has it with your name written on it, waiting for you at the will-call desk. All you have to do is go to the window and ask to receive your ticket.

"Everyone who calls on the name of the Lord will be saved" (Acts 2:21).

Do you have your ticket yet? What are you waiting on? Go and ask for it now.

## Study the Playbook

**READ:** John 3:1–21; Luke 18:13–23; Matthew 10:32

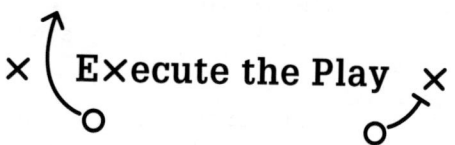

## Execute the Play

If you haven't received Christ as your Savior yet, do that now. If you have, it's important to follow this up with making your decision public. You can declare what Jesus has done for you by getting baptized at your church.

# It's Just a Game

My team lost again. That was it. Our season was done. No playoffs for us. No, I didn't play. Yet, that loss had a huge impact on my frame of mind. Outsiders (those who don't know or love the game) don't have any comprehension of why my team's loss has such an impact on me. I dread facing those people the next day. They tease me and ridicule my team and the game. Sometimes, a bold few have even ventured to rebuke me with the self-righteous phrase, "It's just a game."

Okay. So my team losing isn't the end of the world. But having others belittle or minimize my pain is disconcerting. This is a common aggravation many people share with me, not necessarily regarding a lost football game but a personal hardship or heartache. Something goes wrong at your job, with the children, or in your marriage. You want to share your heartache only to have someone filled with self-proclaimed piety declare that your problem is not grave enough to warrant your sour emotions. Oftentimes, we encounter people wanting to fix, dismiss, or gloss over our troubles.

What causes people to have such a closed-hearted response to us in our time of need? Maybe it's because they have too many burdens in their own lives and feel overwhelmed. Or they might have had a past full of turbulence. But without having gained healing or obtaining healthy, adequate coping skills, these people simply are not equipped to help. Others are too lazy, busy, or self-engrossed to be able to see, much less validate the needs of others.

This isn't the way God intended His children to relate to one another. On the contrary, Paul instructs us to "be happy with those who are happy, and be sad with those who are sad" (Romans 12:15, NCV) and to "carry each other's burdens" (Galatians 6:2).

I might not have the answers to solve a broken heart. But I do know this: if I see you hurting, I'll come alongside and help you carry that burden.

## Study the Playbook

**READ:** Luke 6:38; Hebrews 13:16; 1 John 3:17

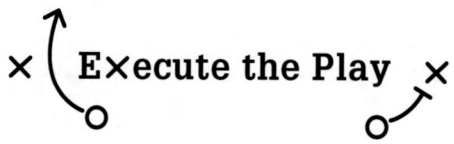

### Execute the Play

Listen to those who share with you their troubles and needs. As you have time and resources, offer to help meet those needs.

# Sideline Saints

Y ou rarely see them. Few people know they exist. There are no autograph sessions, no limelight, no cheering fans, nor any large contracts. Yet, these chosen few go where only the elite trod. They bend the ear of some of the most wealthy and influential men in today's society. Sought out in times of trial and called for in tear-filled moments, these are the sideline saints, the chaplains of the NFL.

What is it to be the spiritual leader to those whom so many idolize? To many of the young players, he is a father figure, guiding, sometimes correcting, but always steadfast. To some of the veterans, he is a counselor who has drawn along side to help bear some of life's burdens. For the old men, he is a comrade in arms, a true friend in the midst of hype and hoax. For the alumni, he is a constant in a world full of change. The NFL chaplain is one man with many different roles. The great evangelist, Paul, understood this multiplicity of tasks. He said, "I have become all things to all men so that by all possible means I might save some" (1 Corinthians 9:22).

The chaplain encounters several types of men. There is a man who, never having come to trust Christ to be his Savior, is full of doubt and distrust. Gently, the chaplain shares the truth of a living, loving Lord. Another man is the Christian who knows the Word but has been caught up by the world. Firmly, this minister reproves him for his stubborn rebellion. And then there is the believer who is weary and battle-worn. Carefully, this shepherd tends to the wounded heart and heavy soul. Finally, we see the mature saint, full of victory and praise. Joyfully, the chaplain joins his co-laborer in the fields of harvest.

Paul reminded us, "How beautiful are the feet of those who bring good news" (Romans 10:15). It is with great honor that I share this tribute of appreciation to all God's servants in the NFL. Chaplain, on behalf of all you serve, thank you.

## Study the Playbook

**READ:** Titus 2:2, 6–8;
Proverbs 17:27; 1Timothy 3:1–7

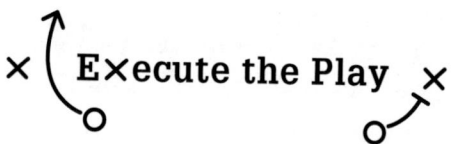

## Execute the Play

Your chaplain or pastor pours out his life to bless yours. Don't wait for a special occasion to show your appreciation. Find out what are his interests and/or needs. Contribute some extra money in the offering plate to bless him specifically. Or maybe buy a gift certificate for the golf course. You might purchase gift cards so he can take his family out to eat and enjoy a movie, too.

Inspired by and dedicated to the memory and legacy of John Weber, former chaplain to the Dallas Cowboys.

# The Cursed Zebra

I f you've been around football very much you've probably developed a strong opinion about the unique breed known as 'The Zebra'. No, I'm not talking about the animal you see in the metropolitan zoo or in Africa. I'm talking about the officials or referees of the game. They are the infamous men running up and down the field whom we just love to hate. We're all convinced that they must be partially blind. I know I've offered (quite loudly to boot) a pair of my glasses to help them with all those missed holding calls. No doubt on more than one occasion they've heard an earful of expletives shouted their direction, from coaches and fans alike.

I've got a theory as to why we are so 'anti' these officials. I think it could be that we just don't like hearing the word *no*. We hate for anyone to correct us when we're wrong. If you think I'm exaggerating then watch a two-year-old when his mother tells him no to getting that toy in the check-out line. Or see how the teen responds when her dad corrects her choice of clothing for the evening. Check out the employee ranting over the boss's micromanagement with his oppressive set of new office rules. And if you want to see a major tantrum, view the scene as the speeding business executive gets pulled over by the motorcycle officer.

Doesn't it just 'chap your emotional hide' to have someone or something block your efforts or goals? I wonder if it has something to do with a desire to have god-like independence. If memory serves me correctly, Eve and Adam had a difficult time accepting God's limited number of rules. They were simple and few, but they were clear, and the consequences were firm. It's just human nature to want to cry out against set rules and create the rules as we go in order to ensure that 'self' wins.

At least we're not the only ones afflicted with this emotional struggle. Apparently, Solomon was familiar with it as well. In Proverbs 14:12 and 16:25, he wrote, "There is a way that seems right to a man, but in the end it leads to death" (Proverbs 14:12).

Unfortunately for all the game's Zebras, and anyone else in a position of authority, these individuals will often encounter a less than friendly welcome. Jesus said that "a prophet is honored everywhere except in his hometown and in his own home" (Matthew 13:57, NCV).

How is it that God would have us respond to those in authority? We are to yield to the leadership of all our rulers. Why? Because "no one rules unless God has given him the power to rule, and no one rules now without that power from God" (Romans 13:1, NCV).

It sure does go against the grain of our flesh. But without the officiating team, the game would become so raucous that it might spur on riots. Without parents, children would be a danger to themselves. Without bosses and supervisors, employees would do very little except pick up a check. Without the police force and the law, our society would run amuck. As we can imagine, without God's establishment of order, there would be chaos. If we are going to be allowed to play the full course of the game, we must be willing to abide by the rules established. In playing the game of life, we must reference and play by the rules written in the Bible. For a quick refresher, I recommend we start with the basics, found in Exodus 20:1–10. Playing by the rules makes for a very challenging and rewarding game. Wouldn't you agree?

## Study the Playbook

READ: 1 Samuel 15:22; Hebrews 13:17; Romans 13:1–7

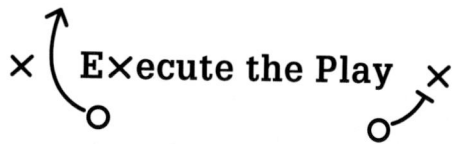

### Execute the Play

Give respect to all who are in authority over you: your boss, the police officer, your pastor and church leaders. Show this honor with your tone of voice, words and actions. Be quick to comply with their directives.

# The Playoffs

For those of us who eat, sleep, and breathe football, the playoffs mark the most wonderful time of the year. We've watched our favorite team battle through a season of sixteen grueling games. For those teams that didn't make the cut, the season has ended. And literally, they are back to the drawing board.

The name really says it all. The *playoffs* are a series of games in which two teams come together with the object to *play* the other team *off* the list of contenders. That translates to being out of the running for the prize: the Super Bowl. It's an incredibly intense time of play. Some teams are eliminated after just one round (game). Only two teams persevere and survive to the final clash: the Super Bowl. They've already been named the champion of their division (area) and conference (semi-national grouping of teams). But all of that glory wanes in the shadow of the elusive and mighty Lombardi (Super Bowl) trophy. The conclusion of the final game brings awesome jubilation to the winners and near-despair for the losing team. The Super Bowl is a mighty creation of the NFL. And yet, with all of its apparent power, prestige, and pull, it is still a game for the entertainment of the masses.

Unfortunately, it seems that many people approach Christianity as if it were the 'playoffs to heaven'. Too many of us have missed the message : God gave us His unconditional love in the form of His Son, Jesus the Christ. Did you catch that all important word *unconditional?* There's not a thing or any task or great work that God requires of us in order to receive His awesome and everlasting love. Yet, we approach God as if we have to play through grueling matches in order to win His approval and love. God isn't playing games. He has birthed us into His kingdom with the gift of salvation through His Son, Jesus.

As family, friends and fans huddle up to catch these exciting games, let's remember that the teams might be played-off but we, as believers, cannot, for we are already born into victory through Christ, our Champion.

> "But God demonstrates his own love for us in this: While we were still sinners, Christ died for us" (Romans 5:8).

> "For it is by grace you have been saved, through faith—and this not from yourselves, it is the gift of God" (Ephesians 2:8).

# Study the Playbook

READ: John 6:37; 2 Timothy 1:9; Romans 8:38–39

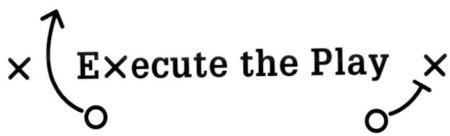

## Execute the Play

When you start to fall prey to thinking that you must earn your way past those pearly gates, read and recite these verses. Keep reading and reciting until they've erased all your doubts. Remember that Jesus has already paid the price for your admission into Heaven.

_____

_____

_____

_____

_____

_____

_____

_____

_____

_____

_____

_____

_____

_____

# True Colors

At the beginning of the season, spirits are as high as the proposed potential of the home team. Every fan can be found sporting team colors. Faces get painted. Homes and cars get decked out in banners and more. Avid fans wear logo jewelry, hats, socks, jerseys, and jackets. Anything and everything that shows team spirit is fair game.

With the first kickoff, speculation and predictions get traded in for reality. That first win just seems to add fuel to the fire that this year will be "the year" for our team. But somewhere down the schedule, a few losses get logged. Hopes aren't as high. Spirits wane. Doubts begin to creep in. Team colors begin to fade from the stands. For some, disappointments and hard times are too rough to endure. Add too many *L's* to that record and some fans jump ship and land on board with a different team. It is then that these fans show their true colors: wishy-washy, yellow.

Turn back time to the day when you trusted Christ as your Savior. You were so gung-ho to live for Jesus. You were hungry to love the Lord, learn of Him, and serve in His kingdom. But somewhere down life's schedule, challenges and losses came into play. Ridicule and persecution tackled you and your dreams. Temptation entered in with the enemy whispering for you to take the easy road to the good life. It wasn't long before it became difficult for spectators to tell whose team you were on.

Hypocrisy is nothing new. John warned the church about hypocrisy. He admonished those early believers to "not love the world or anything in the world. If anyone loves the world, the love of the Father is not in him" (1 John 2:15).

We need to return to our first love, regardless of the losses that have come our way (Revelation 2:1–7). Come on, Christian. The kickoff is upon us. Time to wear our true colors.

## Study the Playbook

**READ:** Matthew 7:21–23, 15:7–9; Proverbs 26:23–26; James 2:14–26

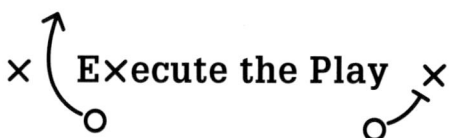

## Execute the Play

Remember how it felt when you first made Jesus the Lord of your life. Return to that level of passion through daily Bible reading, genuine prayer, and weekly fellowship with other growing believers.

# What Will
# You Leave?

M ost of the players who were drafted a decade ago have faded into the sunset of retirement. Most never got a chance to play in the Super Bowl. Only a handful will be inducted into the Hall of Fame. For a few magical years, these men were at the very athletic summit this world has to offer. But those days are over.

Sometimes these former players reflect on what they left behind. Framed articles and plaques of honor hang on the walls. Trophies fill cases. Jerseys and helmets rest in prominent display. Autographed pictures with celebrities and game memorabilia are sprinkled in the midst of these other treasures. Great feats were accomplished and new records were set. But history teaches us that yesterday's accolades are soon forgotten; and records are meant to be broken. What remains that has lasting value? Will these superstars of yesteryear be remembered as men of honor and valor?

Not too long ago, we had the sudden shock of having to bury my mother. Since her death our family has been sorting through Mother's estate. While I was packing away her shoes, I discovered a message she had meant for me. Beyond the tears, I saw that Mother had left behind much more than belongings. The nearly new condition of the shoes reminded me of her lessons of good stewardship. The neat arrangement of the shoes was reminiscent of her value of orderliness. Even though she is gone, I still see evidence of the legacy she left behind. Engraved in every room in the house and in my own reflection, I see the results of those lessons. This ties in with what Paul told Titus to share with the church: "Teach the older women to be reverent in the way they live, not to be slanderers or addicted to much wine, but to teach what is good" (Titus 2:3). My mother's legacy of integrity and godly character lives on in our hearts and lives.

When you walk away from your career, what will you leave behind? When you draw your last breath, what legacy will you have etched into the minds and hearts of those you love? For the sake of their comfort and the glory of God, I pray that you make your life an estate worth passing on to the generations to come.

## Study the Playbook

**READ:** Proverbs 13:22;
Deuteronomy 6:1–7; Romans 8:17

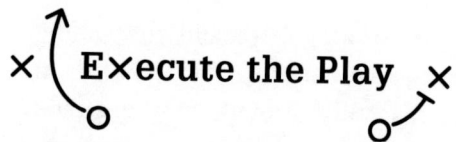

## Execute the Play

If you haven't already started, begin saving for your legacy and your children's future. Model the behavior that you want your children and grandchildren to emulate. Let your actions paint a self portrait you will be proud to leave behind.

_____

_____

_____

_____

_____

_____

_____

_____

_____

_____

_____

_____

_____

_____

# When Fans Meet

Outsiders have no clue what a group of people could possibly find so interesting about this game of football. But for those of us who proudly hold the title of fan, we more than understand. We cherish the game and our status.

So what is it that we do? On game day we tailgate, gather at the local sports restaurant, or meet at the home of one of the faithful, where we slosh down those mouth-watering munchies with our favorite drink while rooting for our team. We compare who has the most team memorabilia, show off our latest in team apparel (officially licensed, of course), and compare who has the greatest number of pictures and autographs. In a word, we brag. We brag about our team, our knowledge of the sport, the plays, the coaches, the players … and, if we dare, the players we know personally. It is a real "ooh, ahh, wow" moment to declare a personal relationship with a player. And the bragging rights escalate to match with his salary and star power. Can you imagine if during one of our game-day gatherings, the star player from our team walked in? There might be a hush and then a clamoring for his attention and autograph. What a perfectly glorious moment of personal triumph you, the fan, would have if this man came directly to you, put his arm around your shoulders, and announced to the huddled mass that he knows you and you know him! Talk about bragging rights. That would be great enough to last a lifetime.

There is a scene even more awesome. Imagine this: Jesus Christ, the Morning Star, walks into the room. The people converge on Him like two linebackers zeroing in on a quarterback. But He cuts through the crowd to get to you. He puts His strong, right arm around your shoulders and boldly announces that He knows you and you know Him. But this story is no fantasy. Jesus promised that this would be our reality if we choose it to be. There is no greater claim to glory than to know Him!

Do you know Jesus or do you just know *about* Him? You can set that record straight today. For heaven's sake, don't walk away until you do.

"I am the good shepherd; I know my sheep and my sheep know me" (John 10:14).

## Study the Playbook

**READ:** John 3:1–18, 10:1–18, 15:15; Zephaniah 3:17

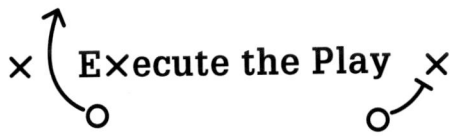

## Execute the Play

If you have received Christ as your personal Savior, you have the best friend of all eternity. Take time, every day, to talk to Him. Thank Him for all He is to you. Thank Him for His love for you.

_____

_____

_____

_____

_____

_____

_____

_____

_____

_____

_____

_____

# A Warrior's Tears

n every battle, there are those who must lead the way. The infantry are the foot soldiers who pave a path to victory. Linemen and blocking backs are the infantry of football. Quiet and unassuming, they often slip into history without being noticed. Yet without their crucial work, the glories of brilliant catches, thrilling runs and dazzling touchdowns would not come to pass.

Let's take a closer look at one of these great warriors. Strong and resolute, he would seem invincible. But when he is battle-worn and standing on the brink of insurmountable odds, silent tears slip down his stubbled cheeks. Still, he remains steadfast. He continues to carry out his mission. He keeps on pressing ahead so that there might be victory at the day's end.

In the church, we have such a soldier. Often unseen and almost always unheralded is the prayer warrior. He takes seriously the charge to "pray without ceasing" (1 Thessalonians. 5:17, NKJV) "as he intercedes for others. He knows that we are to" pray for one another because "the prayer of a godly person is powerful" (James 5:16, NIRV).

At the midnight hour, this warrior weeps bittersweet tears. Bitter because the burden of helping to shoulder the heavy load of another (Galatians 6:2) often seems unbearable. But the tears are also sweet because our soldier knows "the battle is the Lord's" (1 Samuel 17:47).

Victory is certain.

Soldier, thank you for standing in the gap. Your faithfulness is now being heralded by your fellow infantrymen and will one day be rewarded by God, our Commander in Chief.

## Study the Playbook

**READ:** Psalm 4:1, 145:18; Isaiah 55:6; Ephesians 6:18; 1 Timothy 2:1

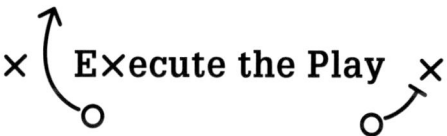

Perhaps you have someone who is faithful to pray for you. Thank that special warrior. Follow their example and stand in the gap for people you know who are in need of that spiritual hedge of protection.

# Cut

Sweat, blood, and tears were your investment. You gave your heart. How many times did you suit up? Did you count the number of team meetings you sat through? Have you added up the injuries you suffered? How many seasons did you play for the team? They called you into the office. Did you see it coming? Were the words fancy and slick or cold and hard? Either way, the message was the same. "Cut from the team," resonated through your mind. Like a broken record, the words kept playing again and again. How could it be? All through the draft, they were the ones who had courted you. They kept saying how much they needed you and wanted you to be a part of their big family. It was quite the seduction. What went wrong? Those stinging tears come from a heart broken under the weight of rejection.

A similar picture is painted in the corporate world each day. One pink slip and all that was familiar becomes history. What seemed sure now becomes a mere vapor. In the matters of the heart, marriages get ripped apart. In other words, people tell others they've been cut. Promises made, dreams woven; yet they were all dashed against the cruel rocks of reality.

Is it any wonder that so many fear reaching out and trusting God? Would He too offer up a bitter cup of rejection after having promised all of heaven?

> Can anything ever separate us from Christ's love? Does it mean He no longer loves us if we have trouble or calamity, or are persecuted, or are hungry or cold or in danger or threatened with death? No, despite all these things, overwhelming victory is ours through Christ, who loved us. And I am convinced that nothing can ever separate us from His love. Death can't, and life can't. The angels can't, and the demons can't. Our fears for today, our worries about tomorrow, and even the powers of hell can't keep God's love away.
>
> Romans 8:35, 37–38 (NLT)

Praise God we will never be cut from God's promises or love.

## Study the Playbook

**READ:** 1 John 4:8; Romans 8:31–32; John 17:23; Jeremiah 31:3

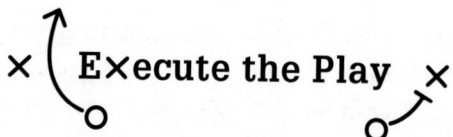

# Execute the Play

You may be feeling sad from experiencing a recent rejection. But never put God in with the group that has turned away from you. Our Father has and always will love you. Daily remind yourself of this truth.

_____

_____

_____

_____

_____

_____

_____

_____

_____

_____

_____

_____

_____

_____

# How Much Is Enough?

I f you keep up with the latest sports news, you know that it's not unusual for a key athlete to hold out on reporting to training camp. Usually it's because the player wants more money. The latest trend is multi-million-dollar contracts. At some point, the question has to be asked, *How much is enough?* One has to wonder how these outrageous contracts help build team spirit. Since when has greed been an asset for cementing a sense of unity?

I'm thinking it would be really wise if team owners would consult the Bible before they toss out so much money. Ironically, God has quite a bit to say about money. In fact, it is the most frequently discussed topic in the Bible. God is concerned that we don't take on the attitude of being self-made. He warns against this attitude and reminds us that it is through His goodness that we prosper, that He is the One who gives us power and wealth. He warns that if there is a focus on self-glory, the power and wealth can and will be taken away.

The dollar amounts of each year's top contracts seem astronomical. It might be easy to sit on the sidelines and judge these star athletes for our presumption of their greed. Yet, this form of pride isn't limited to high-dollar figures. The sin of coveting and selfish ambition can attack at any amount. You see, it's when we begin to trust in our own strength that we become guilty. So just how much is enough? Perhaps we're not asking the right question. Maybe we should be asking, *Who is enough?* The answer is a no-brainer. God is enough. Our assignment then? We are to be diligent to work with all our might to the glory of God and trust Him for our reward.

> You may say to yourself, "My power and the strength of my hands have produced this wealth for me." But remember the LORD your God, for it is he who gives you the ability to produce wealth, and so confirms his covenant, which he swore to your forefathers, as it is today.
>
> Deuteronomy 8:17–18

## Study the Playbook

**READ:** Proverbs 28:22, 25; Luke 12:15; Philippians 2:3

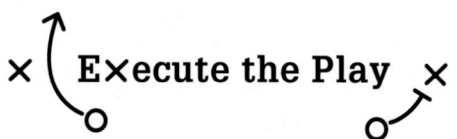

## Execute the Play

Don't worry about what the next person is earning. What you earn is based on your diligence to work and God's faithfulness to bless. Your next assignment is to give thanks to God for His provisions: your ability (talent + education) to work, and the blessing of being gainfully employed.

_____

_____

_____

_____

_____

_____

_____

_____

_____

_____

_____

_____

_____

_____

# The Draft

The season is over, as is the Scouting Combine. In just a matter of days, we will learn of each team's picks.

The players have spent their last season trying to impress the scouts with stellar plays and heroic acts of athleticism. During the Combine, they've pushed their bodies to do the impossible. They've given their all. Why all this press? What prize could be so great as to deserve such a fevered pursuit? It is the prestige, honor, glory, and money that come from playing in the NFL.

The team owners, GM's, coaches, and scouts huddle up in sessions of intense debate over the best investments for the team. Great sums of money and the glory of victory are at stake. Each man wants to say that he was responsible for drafting the stud, not the dud.

And what of the athletes who keep waiting for that special call that never comes? They gave their best, but either it wasn't good enough or they were rejected on a personal level. (After all, there are a limited number

of positions available.) For whatever reason, the draft comes and goes, leaving them out in the cold.

It sounds crazy. Emotions run high. Tension is tight. There is so much on the line. Just an elite few get in. It's ironic. Many people approach heaven and the Christian life the same way. Too many strive to jump through goodness hurdles in order to impress God and make it into heaven. And if they do, they want to make sure they make the elite group of starters. From where did this distorted view of heaven come? How did so many develop such a warped view of God and His love? Jesus has made the truth clear. He said that "no one comes to the Father except through Me" (John 14:6).

But what about those driven individuals who are still convinced that a roster position in heaven has to be earned? God dealt with that too. We are taught that it is "by grace you have been saved, through faith—and this not from yourselves, it is the gift of God—not by works, so that no one can boast" (Ephesians 2:8–9).

Each year we approach the NFL Draft with great anticipation! For the elite few who are chosen, it is great news. For the rest of us, there is even greater news. In God's house, there is no limit of space, no drills or combines, no draft into heaven. There's just a loving Savior bidding all who will to come join His team.

## Study the Playbook

READ: John 3:16;
2 Corinthians 6:2; Romans 5:8, 6:23

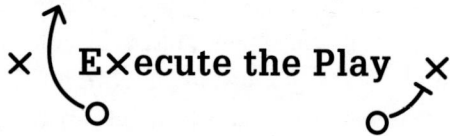

## Execute the Play

Don't wait until you think you're good enough to receive Jesus as your Savior. You don't have to be "good enough" for Him to accept or love you. No more excuses. He's waiting for you to let Him into your life. Open the door to your heart and let Him in. He has drafted you to be on His team!

_____

_____

_____

_____

_____

_____

_____

_____

_____

_____

_____

_____

# Whatever It Takes

A little boy has a dream of playing in the NFL. His parents sign him up for Pee Wee football, take him to all the practices, and encourage him to get back in the game when he is knocked down. In junior high and high school he tries out for the team and makes it. He continues his pursuit of a career in pro ball.

Having worked and played hard, he is offered several college scholarships. Our young man heads off only to be redshirted his first year. Yet he knows he must stay focused and maintain a positive attitude. Beginning his sophomore year, he plays with a fervor that grabs the attention of his coaches, fans, and scouts. Throughout his collegiate career, he spends countless hours working out in the gym. Many nights, he can be found pouring over team notes in his playbook. In the game, he plays hard, pushing himself and his teammates on to excellence. He begins to make and break team records. Soon he catches the attention of the media. Several press releases later and he's gaining the attention of NFL scouts. Soon it's his senior year. He is swarmed by a crowd of media, scouts, and fans at the Scouting Combine and college day. Hype and hysteria swirl around him all the way to the Draft. A wave of relief, excitement, and pride engulf him when he hears his name called.

Having graduated from college, he packs up and heads off to realize his childhood dream of playing in the NFL. Once he gets to training camp he has a dizzying reality check waiting for him. The playbook looks to be twice as big as the Guttenberg Bible, and it's filled with plays so complex that he wonders when they will call him to perform brain surgery. The hits are like everything else at camp: harder. Don't they know it's just practice? But the most difficult adjustment to make is the speed of the game. College was fast, but this pace verges on the brink of breaking the sound barrier. Yet, our young rookie is determined to see his lifetime goal come to pass. He goes early to every practice, works out diligently, and studies up for every team meeting. He has learned that if he's going to be a starter, he has to do whatever it takes. It doesn't take long for the coaches to take notice of this stand-out rookie. Soon, it's the beginning of the season and he runs out of the tunnel, ready to start his first NFL game.

Paul understood this concept of hard work. He said, "Everyone who competes in the games goes into strict training" (1 Corinthians 9:25). For the Christian, God expects and requires this same attitude and action in our pursuit of holiness. Peter coached up the church:

"Prepare your minds for action … just as He who called you is holy, so be holy in all you do" (1 Peter 1:13, 15).

And how do we do that? In God's playbook, we are called to demonstrate holiness by being full of "love, joy, peace, patience, kindness, goodness, faithfulness, gentleness and self control" (Galatians 5:22–23).

Paul said we are to "run in such a way as to get the prize" because it is a "crown that will last forever" (1 Corinthians 9: 24b, 25b).

What do you say? Let's do whatever it takes to be champions for Christ.

## Study the Playbook

**READ:** Philippians 2:12–13;
2 Thessalonians 1:11–12; Hebrews 11:6; James 2:23

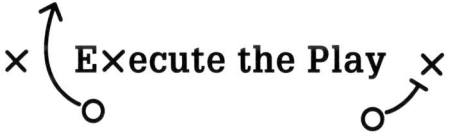

Train hard. Prepare to a standard of excellence in all areas of your life: at home, in the community, on the job, and in your service at church. When it comes time, give your all. Do everything for the glory of God.

# The Price of Looking Back

**W**ith a clear shot and on his way to the end zone, the RB turned to look back over his shoulder. I don't know why. Perhaps he wanted to see if anyone was chasing after him. Unfortunately, that glance backward slowed him down a second or two, just enough to allow his opponent to catch up. The running back's decision to look back cost him a touchdown.

This scene reminds me of an Old Testament story. Take a look at Genesis 19:17. God's angels warned Lot and his family to run. God had reached His limit with the pungent stench of sin from the people of Sodom and Gomorrah. God sent an emergency message: flee or die. (That ought to kick in the afterburners.) There was one little catch: don't look back or you will suffer the same fate as those facing God's wrath. Extended family, house and home, a collection of belongings, social status, a way of life: leave it all behind! Somehow, it must have seemed too great a loss for Lot's wife to leave without one last look back. She turned. The price? More than a touchdown. It cost her life (Genesis 19:26).

What about you? Me? From what must we turn ?

- A familiar sin?

- An affair with an addiction?

- Past successes?

- A Super Bowl ring from years ago?

- Last quarter's promotion?

- An idolatrous love for accolades and adulation?

Whether wrong or right, bad or good, we lose ground for future successes when we look back. From his own personal experience, Paul gave us good advice.

"Forgetting what is behind and straining toward what is ahead, I press on toward the goal to win the prize for which God has called me heavenward in Christ Jesus" (Philippians 3:13:-14).

Friend, look ahead and press on. Victory is just a few yards ahead.

## Study the Playbook

READ: Genesis 19:1–29;
Matthew 7:7–14; Hebrews 12:1–3

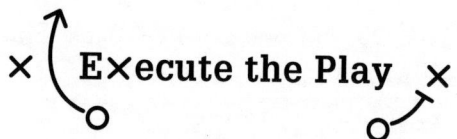

## Execute the Play

Take your focus off all that is holding you back. It's time to break up with that pet sin. And it's time to end your celebration of past glories. Place your attention and energies, instead, on Jesus and living with and for Him.

_____

_____

_____

_____

_____

_____

_____

_____

_____

_____

_____

_____

_____

# A Washed-up Has-been

Retired or released-the reasons may be different, but the end result is the same: you're finished. When the next season starts up, you're no longer watching from the sidelines. No longer do you throw on your helmet as you run onto the field. No. It's over. Now you're just like Joe and Judy Fan, watching the game from your living room sofa. Crushing, isn't it?

The commercials come. You get up to go to the kitchen to get another drink and a few more munchies. That's when you get sucker-punched. With vengeance, your fiendish foe, Satan, has returned. He hits you with his hellish accusations. "You're washed up. You're a has-been. No one remembers you. No one cares about you. See, the phone doesn't ring. Reporters don't come around. No one wants you anymore." Stunned by the blows, you stagger back to the living room. Your family looks at you with questioning eyes. You look beat. You feel as if The Steel Curtain just crashed down on your back. The center snaps the ball, and the family's scrutinizing gaze turns back to the game. Thankful, you sink down in your favorite chair and wonder, *Will the pain ever end? Will the self-doubts and cruel accusations ever stop?*

Friend, why did you let someone else determine your worth? Why did you allow a company to define your identity? You're not alone. We all seem to fall into that trap from time to time. Think back to when we were children. Relatives and family friends would come over, pinch your cheeks, and ask you, "What do you want to be when you grow up?" Right from the beginning it's as if we're programmed to define our value and true self by our vocation. If you think you're free of that now, then take this test. Next time someone asks you what you do, see how you answer. "I'm a linebacker." "I'm a lawyer." "I'm a broker." "I'm a dentist." We tend to answer the question by saying we are what we do. Crazy, isn't it?

Next time our enemy attacks you with an identity crisis, use these as your defense arsenal:

- I'm royalty ... a child of the King! (Galatians 4:4–7)

- I'm a new creature in Christ! (2 Corinthians 5:17)

- I am more than a conqueror! (Romans 8:37)

Friend, wield your sword. These onslaughts of truth will eject your enemy from the game!

# Study the Playbook

**READ:** John 1:12; Romans 5:1;
Colossians 1:13–14; Hebrews 4:14–16

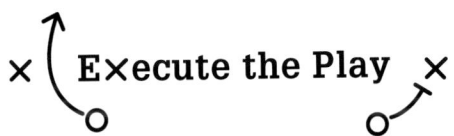

## Execute the Play

Just like you wouldn't allow a stranger to assault you, stop giving the enemy permission to bully you. Block his punches with the powerful word of God. Quit choosing to believe his empty lies. Rather, decide-right now-to believe what God says about you.

_____

_____

_____

_____

_____

_____

_____

_____

_____

_____

_____

# The Legend of the Star

There are a few people who are so magnificent in their field that they earn the title of legend. Rarer yet are the ones who achieve such status while living. One of these is the man with the rifle arm and heart of gold. I'm speaking of Hall of Famer, Roger Staubach.

Many fans of the game can develop a strong, perhaps even fierce, loyalty to their home team. Rival teams and players are often spoken of with a low growl. Yet, when the conversation turns to Roger, there is a respect that almost approaches reverence. This intense competitor earned a deep appreciation throughout the league. I believe it was due to his high standards both on and off the field. His work ethic has been matched only by an elite few. His durability and toughness were a big part of his trademark. All that Roger did, he did with all his heart.

In our daily lives we too are called to exemplify this type of total commitment. Paul taught the Colossians (and us):

Whatever you do, work at it with all your heart, as working for the Lord, not for men, since you know that you will receive an inheritance from the Lord as a reward. It is the Lord Christ you are serving.

Colossians 3:23–24

Perhaps we will not ever hear a packed stadium roar with cheers. We might never see our names and faces glorified on jerseys and trading cards. But through a life committed to living wholly for Christ, we can win the respect of friend and foe for the glory of God.

## Study the Playbook

**READ:** 2 Corinthians 13:11; James 2:14–26

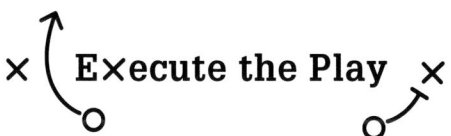

## Execute the Play

Choose to have a mindset of dedication in your preparation. Commit to standards of excellence. Seek to earn and direct all the glory for God. He will make sure He honors and rewards you for your faithful life of service.

# When Eagles Flocked

**M**any of us have grown up with images of a lone eagle soaring through the air, majestic and powerful, with grace and strength intertwining. For just a few moments, I would like to share another picture, one when eagles flocked over one of their own.

August 6, Canton, Ohio. The kickoff to the 2006 season began at the Hall of Fame Game. The Raider Nation had sailed from their Black Hole to meet the Eagles, who had flown from their Philly nest.

To the casual fan, this was pre-season. It was a time to check out the new faces and see what the rookie talent had to offer. Maybe not the top level of game playing; but still, it was the sweet, first rain of football after the drought of the off-season. While you and I might have this viewpoint, no one told Raiders rookie Timi Wusu. With less than two minutes left in the game and eager to make a name (and roster spot) for himself, Timi put a hit that knocked the feathers off Eagles RB Bruce Perry. Time came to a crashing halt as both teams took a knee during this injury time out. It was as if time stood still as Perry continued to lay motionless on the turf. Players urgently motioned for the team doctor. Soon, a medical team huddled around this fallen Eagle. As time dragged on and there was still no movement from Perry, a heavy silence draped the stadium. Doubts and fears took flight in our minds. While many of us began to fear the worst, something strange and wonderful began to take place. One Eagle fell prostrate on the field. Another knelt, with his head to the ground. Soon, there was a flock of Eagles encircling their wounded RB. What began as a heavy silence turned into a holy hush as the stadium was transformed into a cathedral of prayer. Men of great strength were bowed humbly before their holy and mighty God. They were crying out to Jehovah-Rapha, the God of healing, pleading for Him once more to raise up one who was broken. The stretcher and cart came out. Carefully, the medical team lifted and strapped Perry onto the board. As he was being carted off the field to the waiting ambulance, he gave a thumbs-up signal; and hope began to fly in our hearts. Play resumed, but the game had lost a lot of its luster and punch as its significance had paled against the backdrop of mortality.

Just think. This injury timeout became a perfect portrait of intercessory prayer. The Bible tells us that, "The prayer of a righteous man is powerful and effective" (James 5:16).

We are told to come alongside one another during times of sorrow and tribulation. Illness, unemployment, death, divorce, bankruptcy, and brokenness—trials and tests are certain to come our way. These heartaches can seem overwhelming and insurmountable. If we stand alone, they will over power us. Yet it is when we are feeling helpless and hopeless that we must remember we have a powerful ally: prayer. Are you feeling burdened? Come and pray with me.

## Study the Playbook

**READ:** 1 John 5:14–15;
Philippians 4:6–7; Ephesians 6:18

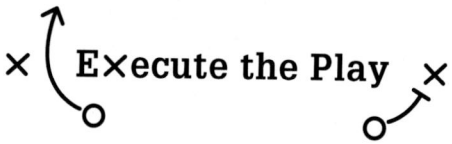

## Execute the Play

The best way to tackle your problems is through prayer. Don't think of prayer as passive, weak and a last resort. Talk to God when life has dealt you a rough blow. Ask and trust Him to see you through to victory and peace.

Note: Bruce Perry suffered a concussion, but thankfully the neck X-rays were negative and the CT scan was normal. He regained feeling and movement in his arms and legs. He was back in the lineup for the season opener.

# All Day

**B**efore a game, teammates gather into a sideline huddle. Soon, they're swaying, chanting, and jumping en mass. The purpose is to encourage one another to give his best and capture victory for the day. One phrase that is commonly heard at that time and throughout the game is, "All day." An explosive message packed into two small words. The players are charging each other to persevere, to keep on when every fiber in their bodies begs to quit. Keep blocking all day. Keep tackling all day. Keep running all day. Keep passing all day. Keep catching all day. Keep kicking all day. Keep scoring all day. Do your job all day. It is a message worth repeating. That's why it's heard over and over on the sidelines, on the field, in the tunnel, and in the locker room.

Weariness is nothing new to this world. Paul had to encourage the Christians at the church in Galatia. He challenged them:

"Don't get tired of doing what is good. Don't get discouraged and give up, for we will reap a harvest of blessing at the appropriate time" (Galatians 6:9, NLT).

Beat to the core, you're thinking of quitting. Day after day, the demands of life pound on your soul. Dirty diapers, business reports, counseling sessions, home repairs, business trips, doctor appointments, papers to grade, bills to pay: life feels so overwhelming. You feel like you're fighting a losing battle. Your body is exhausted, and your soul is weary. Call out to God. Let Him remind you that you are more than a conqueror (Romans 8:37). Let your heavenly Father encourage you to keep on keeping on all day.

## Study the Playbook

**READ:** Philippians 4:13; 2 Chronicles 15:7; Proverbs 23:18; Lamentations 3:22–23

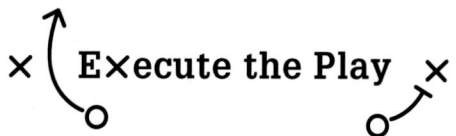

## E×ecute the Play

To be able to keep on keeping on, you must take good care of yourself. Get the rest and proper nutrition necessary to restore your health and energy. Do everything you can to protect and nurture your health. As you crawl into bed, remember, God's strength and mercies will be new each morning.

# When Will They Ever Give It a Rest?

All-American, clean-cut, well-mannered, and talented to boot: Tony Romo. His career was flying to new heights, but … During the pregame of what seemed to be each and every game, the announcers couldn't help but revisit the infamous bobbled snap that ended the Cowboys 2006 season. They've pondered and conjectured a variety of different angles of how that one sour event might hinder or even cripple the remainder of Tony's career. To his many fans, he is the answer to their QB prayers. But to many broadcasters, he is the favorite whipping boy. Those of us who cheer him on to further success echo the thought, *When will they ever give it a rest?*

Many of us can relate to Tony. Not necessarily on the gridiron, but definitely in the game of life. There may be large blunders you've committed that cause you to want to crawl under the nearest rock. Or it could be there are past sins that slink around your soul that cause you to shudder each time you think of them. You're not alone. If we are honest, most of us would confess a similar history. If so many of us suffer with this kind of trauma, why is it that we get bombarded by a fleet of attacks from those around us?

I think the answer lies in one word: *grace.* Those who are bound with a critical spirit either haven't received God's grace or else they don't understand how it is applied. They forget that "no one will be declared righteous in His sight by observing the law; rather, through the law we become conscious of sin" (Romans 3:20).

The good news is the application of grace.

"And *(all)* are justified freely by His grace through the redemption that came by Christ Jesus, (italics mine, Romans 3:24).

Now let's go back to the original question. When will they ever give it a rest? Honestly, your guess is as good as mine. They might never give grace to Tony, just as your tormentors might never grant you any reprieve. Think your sins are too great for God to ever give it a rest? The Psalmist answers this best: "As far as the east is from the west, so far has He removed our transgressions from us" (Psalm 103:12).

## Study the Playbook

READ: Ephesians 4:1–16, 29–32; Proverbs 10:19; James 3:10

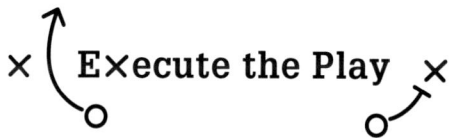

## Execute the Play

Abide by the old saying: if you don't have something good to say, then don't say anything. Look for the good in people. At home or work, catch them doing their tasks well and then give the gift of genuine praise. Express your appreciation of others and their efforts. Use your words to build and restore.

_____

_____

_____

_____

_____

_____

_____

_____

_____

_____

_____

_____

_____

_____

_____

_____

# All That Glistens

One of my favorite channels is the NFL Network. All day, every day, it's all about football. For the wanna-be player relegated to fan-only status, it's as close as we can get to being in the game without actually playing. Needless to say, I park in front of the tube to enjoy all the juicy morsels it has to offer.

As fans, we love to watch the game, collect trading cards, licensed merchandise, and autographs. If you're like the majority of fans, you find yourself glamorizing their world. I know I do. It's hard not to. NFL films pull out the best highlights from the week's games, edit them, and add an array of special effects, not forgetting to use slow motion and music that would stir up any armchair quarterback. They even make a sweating lineman look glamorous!

All that glistens is *not* gold. The sweat from that lineman sure does glisten (especially in slow motion) but I can guarantee it is not gold (nor does it smell like a bouquet of roses). This glamorizing and romanticizing of others is not unique to the world of football. Judging by the sales of tabloids, a majority of people struggle with this same issue. Now, before we think better of ourselves, let's not limit this investigation to sports fans, swooning teens, and bored housewives. A closer look tells us that the business elite can idolize the tycoons in fortune. It would appear that each major profession can boast of their own stars with a loyal entourage of followers.

Apparently, the character flaw of partiality has been evident in people for a very long time. It seems that the first-century and modern-day churches have struggled with this same faulty focus. Listen to the warning James issued:

> Never think some people are more important than others. Suppose…you show special attention to the one…What are you doing? You are making some people more important than others…But if you treat one person as being more important than another, you are sinning.
>
> James 2:1–9 (NCV)

Conclusion? Enjoy the game and appreciate the players. Bless everyone you come in contact with, but exalt Jesus and Jesus only.

# Study the Playbook

**READ:** Acts 10:34–35; Galatians 3:28; Exodus 20:3–6

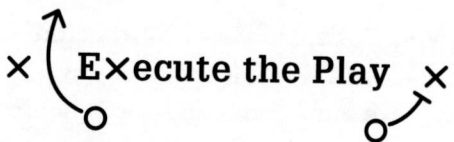

## Execute the Play

Worship belongs to God and Him alone. Be careful that your admiration of others never surpasses your adulation of God!

_____

_____

_____

_____

_____

_____

_____

_____

_____

_____

_____

_____

_____

_____

_____

# Down for the Count?

I f you're like me, you enjoy watching the defensive back hammer his opponents to the ground. When he puts a hit on his intended target, that man is often down for the count. Sometimes, it can feel as if life has hit us so hard that we too are down for the count. Unemployment robs the employee and leaves the bank account and self-esteem empty. Divorce devastates the souls of those who had pledged eternal love to one another. Addictions attack the essence of the one caught in its lethal trap. And death can paralyze those left in its wake of grief. These burdens and the sorrows they bring can tempt even the strongest man to give in and stay down.

When we are in these lows of life, it can feel as if we are the only one experiencing such loss. Friend, take comfort. You are not alone in your suffering. The great Apostle Paul knew what it was like to be knocked down. He told the church in Corinth, "We are hard pressed on every side, but not crushed; perplexed but not in despair; persecuted, but not abandoned; struck down, but not destroyed" (2 Corinthians 4:8–9).

Vince Lombardi, the great Packers coach, once said, "It's not whether you get knocked down. It's whether you get up." What a powerful statement. Within those words is an inherent challenge to get up and finish the game. Paul issued a similar challenge to the Corinthian Christians.

"We do not lose heart … we fix our eyes not on what is seen, but on what is unseen. For what is seen is temporary, but what is unseen is eternal" (2 Corinthians 4:16,18).

He further urges us all to "press on toward the goal to win the prize" (Philippians 3:14). Why continue to wrestle with the traumas and troubles this world dishes out? Paul answers that question with his own life's testimony.

"I do not run like a man running aimlessly; I do not fight like a man beating the air" (1 Corinthians 9:26).

Paul continues to charge us to "fight the good fight of faith" so that we may "take hold of the eternal life to which *(we)* were called" (1 Timothy 6:12). Friend, has life knocked you down? Then take my hand, get up, and together we will continue to "fight the good fight."

## Study the Playbook

**READ:** Psalm 31:24; Proverbs 23:18; Jeremiah 17:7; Philippians 4:6–8

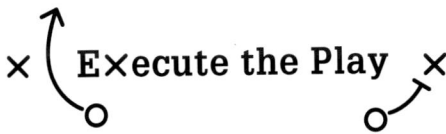

## Execute the Play

On days when there doesn't seem to be any sunshine and you can't even buy a smile, you must determine that you will continue the good fight. Write down seven blessings God has brought into your life. Focus on remembering all the good God has and is doing in your life.

# Without Regard

Think about the league's different head coaches, past and present. Of the many, Bill Parcells has often been considered to be one of the most independent in his thinking. In numerous interviews, he's been very clear in communicating that he's not motivated by what others think of him. At a time when so many are driven to win the approval of others, Coach Parcells stands out as a rather unique man. Without regard to popular opinion, he is a man free to think for himself and free to act according to truth rather than the tyranny of feelings or what others may be saying.

Every teenager knows the angst of going against popular opinion. Not many teenagers want to stand out. It seems easier to go along with the crowd. It's not much different in the adult world. Ask the factory worker under pressure to join the local chapter of the union. Or interview the new secretary if it's easy for her to resist the pressure to chime in on office gossip. Ask any doctor about the regular "invitations" to "support" a new medicine by one of the friendly pharmaceutical companies. Watch the young mother being pressured by a host of "helpful" women, urging her to parent according to their experience. Look at the new husband being harassed to go along with the guys to the local bar for a few drinks before going home.

Whatever our station in life, we will face a variety of temptations to fit in with the crowd. "They" claim to have the answers for all of life's questions. In return for our loyal trust, "they" promise clarity of purpose and a sense of significance. In the end, their empty lies only leave us feeling wounded and betrayed.

Though it appears to be emotional suicide, there is freedom in standing for what is right, even when it means standing alone. Just as Coach Parcells has learned to not allow others to dictate his life, it was a lesson that the Colossian Christians needed to learn as well. Paul instructed them, "Whatever you do, work at it with all your heart, as working for the Lord, not for men" (Colossians 3:23).

It was and still is the only way to have freedom: Live for Christ and Him alone.

## Study the Playbook

**READ:** Galatians 1:10; John 5:41–44; Matthew 6:5, 33

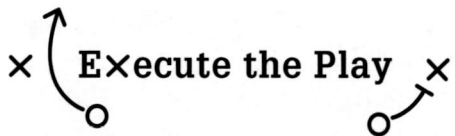

## Execute the Play

Don't pursue the approval of people. Their applause and adoration is fleeting. Instead, make it your sole ambition to win the praise of God. Graciously receive compliments from those who admire you. But without regard for what others may say, base your worth only on what God thinks of you.

_____

_____

_____

_____

_____

_____

_____

_____

_____

_____

_____

_____

# An Empty Shell

Thousands would drive by, but it was no longer alive with activity. There were no fans clamoring to get into its gates. All the seats, concession stands, equipment, and amenities had been removed. Essentially, it had been gutted and was waiting for the demolition crews to come and put it to rest. In many ways, it was rather depressing to look at the old stadium. What used to be so full of life was just a reminder of days gone by. It was an empty shell of what once was.

This triggers memories of when I stood over my father's casket. I looked at the eyes that used to gaze lovingly at me now closed in death. I looked at the hands folded peacefully that used to guide and protect me. I looked at that head that had been so full of wisdom and truth now still on the casket pillow. I looked in only to see an empty shell of the man I used to call Daddy.

Before I wax too sorrowful, let me review with you the other side of truth and its friend, hope. We realize that in order to experience the glories of all the tomorrows to come, our team had to leave the old stadium behind. We could not receive nor accommodate all that the owner had in store for the team and fans in that old place. It's the same way with us. Paul reminds us that our spirits, which are made in the image of God (Genesis 1:26–27), are treasures stored in a jar of clay (2 Corinthians 4:7). The Owner of our soul has such glorious plans for us in heaven, but our earthly bodies are incapable of accommodating all that God wants to give to us. In order for us to receive all that He has stored up for us, we must leave this old body behind. God has given us "an inheritance that can never perish, spoil or fade … kept in heaven" (1 Peter 1:4).

While I'm still here on earth, I might shed another tear or two as I miss loved ones who've gone on ahead of me. But I will hold strong to the hope that I too will one day rejoice with them in a brilliant place called glory.

## Study the Playbook

**READ:** Psalm 16:11; John 14:1–3; Philippians 3:20–21; Revelation 21

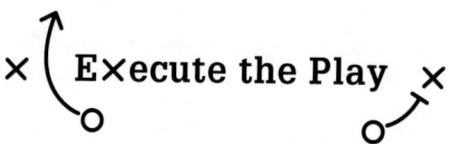

As you grieve the death of a loved one, also keep in mind the joys and blessings they are now able to enjoy to the fullest. Think about how you will be able to join them some day. Envision what a glorious reunion that will be!

Let this be a motivation and encouragement to live your life in such a way that it will be a tribute to our Lord and your loved ones.

# Words to Live By

Plastered throughout the Oakland Raiders stadium are these words: "Commitment to Excellence." These are more than just words to owner, Al Davis. They represent more than a mindset. One could say that these words are a way of life for this man.

Almost every team-whether high school, collegiate, or pro-has a team motto designed to motivate them to play their way to victory. Some have the habit of touching and/or reciting those words as they enter the locker room, walk onto the field, or work out in the weight room. Wherever they go, the purpose is to embed those words so deeply into the player's minds that they become part of the man himself.

There is power in words. Think about it. Many churches recite their confession of faith as part of their worship service. Almost every recovery group begins their meetings with a confession statement. Numerous self-help groups and seminars also recognize the power of the spoken word. If you're familiar with pop psychology, you've heard the phrases "self-talk" and "daily affirmation." Though many people today think that they've discovered something new and innovative, they might be surprised to learn that the Bible had something to say about the power of words thousands of years ago. The wisest man our planet has known penned, "The tongue has the power of life and death" (Proverbs 18:21). King Solomon knew how important it is for our words to be positive and purposeful.

Here's my point. You have a motto you live by. Think not? Ask those closest to you to describe the way you live. Whether you've thought it out or not, you are living out what you truly believe. Don't like the message you're sending out? Here's some good news. You have the power to change it. Start speaking powerful words of life and start living right now.

## Study the Playbook

**READ:** James 3:2; Ephesians 4:29; Colossians 3:16; Matthew 15:11; Proverbs 13:3

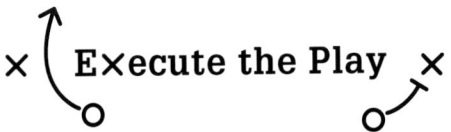

### Execute the Play

Your tongue is incredibly powerful! Learn to give yourself a halftime pep talk. Recite Scripture that reminds you who God is, how wonderful He is and how important you are to Him.

# The Turf's Greener

t's amazing. Pick up the morning paper. Look at the sports section. Another player is asking to be traded to another team. Perhaps he's past his prime, but he doesn't think so. He doesn't want to be relegated to second string. So he asks to be traded. Surely another team will pay and appreciate him more by giving him more playing time. In his mind, the turf is definitely greener on the other side.

Now pick up that same paper a year later. Yes, he was traded. They had offered him more money. And yes, he did get to start. But he wasn't appreciated any more. And now his new team has begun to discuss moving him to the dreaded second string. What was so enticing not too long ago has become very disappointing. Disillusionment sets in. This wasn't the way he had seen the story play out in his mind.

If you think this doesn't apply to you, then try this scenario on for size. Your spouse doesn't look quite as winsome as the day you two walked down the aisle. Years and gravity have taken their toll. Chores and responsibilities seem to be all that tops your conversation charts. Life seems dull, boring, and unfulfilling. You feel unappreciated. You begin to think there might be a more exciting life elsewhere. Now without realizing it, your heart and mind are open to that possibility.

How ironic. Pretty soon, a young DDG (drop-dead gorgeous) new employee just so happens to be one of your new co-workers. The desire to have a more exciting and fulfilling life begins to consume your thoughts. You kick into action and begin to pursue that forbidden relationship. It appears to be more rewarding—no chores, no responsibilities. Open schedules quickly lead to open arms. Soon, this new life takes off at a dizzying speed. You feel excited and appreciated.

Now pick up next year's paper. Oh yes. That's your garage sale. And look. The house is for sale too. Guess all that came about when your spouse learned of your adulterous affair. Oh, and I guess that would be your name in the divorced column.

Statistics show that more than 50 percent of today's marriages end in divorce. And even higher numbers are posted for extra-marital affairs. But God never intended for us to ever experience infidelity or divorce. He made His thoughts clear to us:

"Marriage must be respected by all, and the marriage bed kept undefiled, because God will judge immoral people and adulterers" (Hebrews 13:4, HCSB).

In light of this understanding, let me recommend that we not fall prey to the devious scheme that the turf's greener on the other side. I don't know about yours, but mine's looking pretty green.

# Study the Playbook

**READ:** Genesis 2:23;
Galatians 3:28; Ephesians 5:21–33

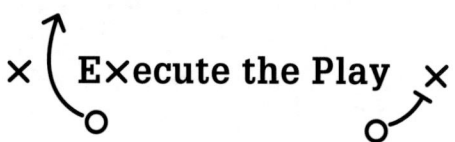

## Execute the Play

Your marriage is valuable. Invest into it. Set a regular time to spend time with your spouse. Guard it jealously. Take each other out for a date. Discover and develop a mutually enjoyable hobby. Read the Bible and pray together. Honor one another by striving to meet the other's needs. Don't even think of asking for a trade: strive to *keep your own turf green!*

_____

_____

_____

_____

_____

_____

_____

_____

_____

# Are You Ready?

**F**or the remainder of the winter, all of spring, and through the unbearable heat of summer, we've waited to hear those beautiful words. Go ahead, finish the question. Yes, that's it! *"Are You Ready for Some Football?" It's the first game of the season. Let's go through the checklist.

- Favorite snack? *Check.*

- Favorite drink? *Check.*

- Favorite group of fans (to share in the joys of victory or the agony of defeat)? Check.

- Remote? *Check.*

- Cordless phone (should anyone be so unsavvy as to call during the game)? *Check.* (Might let the answering machine catch those. That's what the machine is for, right?)

- Sports section of the newspaper (for cross-referencing stats)? *Check.*

- Bad call 'brick' (to throw at the TV)? *Check.*

- Favorite team pillow and blanket? *Check.*

Great! Now, let's look in the mirror and make sure we're dressed for the game. Yep, we've got our team hat, jersey, socks, and team-colored shoes. We're ready.

It's funny what great lengths we go to in order to get ready to watch a game on the tube. What if we posed the question a bit differently? What if the question asked about our readiness to live a Christ-like life? What would that check list look like?

- Daily Bible reading?
- Personal prayer life?
- Regular attendance and service in a local church?
- Christian friends (for support and accountability)?
- Faithful tithing?
- Submission to authority?
- Kind and respectful in speech and action to all?

To how many could we answer *"Check"?* This list isn't intended to place anyone on a guilt trip. But it is meant to be a reminder to stretch ourselves to live a life of readiness to serve and obey Christ. Paul encouraged Timothy and multiple generations of readers when he wrote, "Be diligent to present yourself approved to God, a worker who does not need to be ashamed, rightly dividing the word of truth" (2 Timothy 2:15, NKJV).

Be encouraged. Now let's get ready.

# Study the Playbook

**READ:** Luke 9:23; 2 Timothy 3:16–17; James 1:22–25

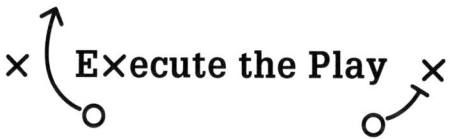

## Execute the Play

Follow and apply yourself to the Christ-like life checklist. Be intentional. Purpose in your heart and mind that you will live in such a way that others will shout their cheers for Christ.

*"Are You Ready for Some Football"
written and recorded by Hank Williams, Jr.

_____

_____

_____

_____

_____

_____

_____

_____

_____

_____

_____

# The Seedy Side

S ad to say, but it seems like every honorable profession has a dark side to it. And the world of football is no exception. One of the rotten apples in the game's barrel is gambling. For those of us who are naive, it almost seems sacrilege to think it goes on in our favorite world. Yet gambling in sports is big business.

A recent movie, *Two for the Money*, deals with this matter. Perhaps the purpose in making the movie was to shed light on a dark subject. If so, I wonder if this wake-up call made a difference.

Driven by greed, there are some who would like to tell us that we are of no value without the high dollars and high stakes. Another sports-related film has coined the phrase, "Show me the money." Is the value of life and a person's worth really measured in the green and silver of our bank accounts?

I can't think of a better place to turn for truth than the Bible. Even in those ancient times, people yearned for the good life.

"You want something but don't get it. You kill and covet, but you cannot have what you want. You quarrel and fight. You do not have, because you do not ask God. When you ask, you do not receive, because you ask with wrong motives, that you may spend what you get on your pleasures" (James 4:2–3)

Whether driven by the hunger for another thrilling adrenaline rush or the intoxicating promise of large sums of cash, for some it is too easy to wade into the snare of gambling. Yet, the lure was a mirage that disguised a fortified dungeon. Friend, there is hope. The Bible has a plan of escape to offer the prisoner.

"Two are better than one, because they have a good return for their work: If one falls down, his friend can help him up. But pity the man who falls and has no one to help him up! Also, if two lie down together, they will keep warm. But how can one keep warm alone? Though one may be overpowered, two can defend themselves. A cord of three strands is not quickly broken" (Ecclesiastes 4:9–12)

There are support groups available to help you escape this tormenting prison. In addition to attending a group, it will help to have a trusted friend who will love and hold you accountable through this journey out of the gambling addiction.

Whether you have or have not taken that downward plunge into the world of gambling, it is helpful to weigh the cost. Look at Jesus's philosophy regarding greed:

"What kind of deal is it to get everything you want but lose yourself? What could you ever trade your soul for?" (Matthew 16:26, MSG).

Everything I want- for the price of my soul? No thanks. Those stakes are too steep for me!

## Study the Playbook

**READ:** 1 Timothy 6:9–10; Proverbs 13:11; Matthew 6:24; Ecclesiastes 4:10; 1 Corinthians 6:12

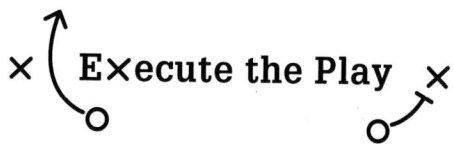

## Execute the Play

If you have an addiction to gambling, look in the mirror and admit this truth to yourself. Your next step is to seek godly counsel. A Christian counselor would be a good option. You can also look into joining a support group. Your church may have a recovery program. Or you can join the local chapter of Gambler's Anonymous. To find out when and where they are meeting, call 213–386–8789 or log on to www.gamblersanonymous.org.

# Wrap 'Em Up, Boys

Is there anything quite as exciting as watching a linebacker eat a QB sandwich? It's one of my favorites to watch. I can't help but hit that DVR replay button a couple more times. But for all the enjoyments we have watching this glorious moment, those linebackers spend hours practicing a simple task: the art of wrapping up the tackle. It's not uncommon to hear the defensive coordinator barking out the command to 'wrap 'em up'. When a quarterback has dropped out of the pocket, he knows he's running for his life. A simple, one-handed grab won't be enough to bring down today's QB. And the only thing a single forearm will bring is a possible cast on a broken bone. No. The coach is wise in teaching his players to wrap two arms around the fleeing opponent, drop him, and walk away. When executed properly, this tackle brings a war hoop from the stands and jubilance from his teammates. But a missed tackle leaves the 'boos' from our fans accompanying the other team's touchdown resonating all the way down to the LB's cleats.

Today men are facing a moral dilemma that seems as elusive to tackle as the most fleet-footed quarterback on the loose: internet pornography. In a recent poll, 61 percent of Christian men admitted to having some involvement with the sin of internet porn.* The Bible gives a powerful and strict warning: flee youthful lust. For too many men, it only takes one look and the battle is lost. Paul coached men to "take captive every thought to make it obedient to Christ" (2 Corinthians 10:5).

In other words, each man is to handle pornographic material and lust the same way those linebackers handle that scrambling quarterback.

1. Wrap it up.

2. Slam it down. (DeMarcus-Ware-style)

3. Walk away.

Listen. The angels are cheering you on your best tackle yet.

## Study the Playbook

**READ:** Matthew 5:28; 1 John 2:16;
1 Corinthians 6:18–20; Hebrews 13:4; Philippians 4:8

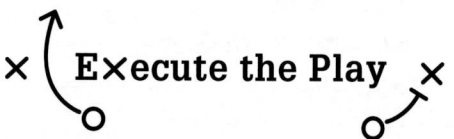

## Execute the Play

Tackle this monster before it destroys you and your family! Get an honest man to be your accountability/prayer partner. Do NOT miss meeting with him every week. Find a Christian counselor who will help you rebuild your marriage. Join a support group. To check for the Every Man's Battle Support Group in your area, call 800-NEW-HOPE (800–639–4673).

*(*Every Man's Battle* by Stephen Arterburn and Fred Stoeker)

# Authentic and Officially Licensed

Walk into any NFL team pro shop and you will be overwhelmed by the variety of merchandise all sporting the team name or logo. On display are T-shirts, jerseys, jackets, and a variety of clothing for men, women, and children. They even have togs for babies and pets. You can find an abundance of footballs, miniature helmets, doormats, board games, mugs, steins, glasses, hats, blankets, and pens. Or you can buy autographed pictures, sunglasses, teddy bears, bobble heads, dolls, or baby bottles. You get the idea. Just about everything you can imagine, and it all shouts team spirit. And somewhere on the item or price tag will be a small, circular, holographic sticker that indicates that it is authentic and officially licensed.

Team owners and commercials coach us to "wear what the pros wear." Fans are warned against purchasing "autographed" photographs without this seal. Sadly, too many money-hungry scavengers have cashed in by swindling a loyal fan-based mar-

ket with forged signatures. Some fans are ridiculed when sporting knock-offs of authentic team apparel and merchandise. It's obvious that the majority of fans want to identify with their team, but not all are willing to pay the price for the legit product.

Many in the church seem to follow these same patterns. Some are careful to stay within biblical doctrine. They recognize and want to identify with the real deal. They are careful to stay clear of imitations. Sadly, others are easily lured away with teachings that tickle the ears and require little cost or sacrifice. They fall prey to those who would swindle their souls to make a fast buck. Cults promise the world and heaven to boot. But in the end, all they can deliver is a one-way ticket to hell. What appeared to be a small price tag ends up being one that burns the shirt off the back of the one fooled. Over and over, the Scriptures warn us of false prophets who would lead the weak-minded into false teachings. Jesus Himself was adamant when He told the early church to beware of those who would come along with the purpose of deceiving many.

So, whether shopping for your next team jersey or looking for your new church home, make sure you get the real deal by choosing the one with the Owner's authentic and officially licensed seal.

"Watch out that no one deceives you. For many will come in my name, claiming, 'I am the Christ,' and will deceive many" (Matthew 24:4–5).

# Study the Playbook

**READ:** 1 John 4:1–6; Matthew 7:15; Romans 16:17–18

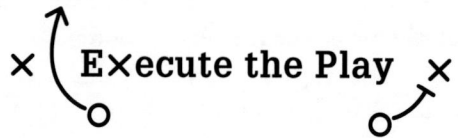

Study the Bible, so you will be able to recognize the lies when they are presented. Spend time talking and listening to God. This way, you'll be able to distinguish between the enemy and your Father's voice. Study what is real and true, so that you will be able to reject what is dangerous and false.

_____

_____

_____

_____

_____

_____

_____

_____

_____

_____

# The Shame of It All

The headlines scream of yet another NFL player caught in a web of scandal—drugs, illicit sex, violence, speeding car chases, fortunes blown, theft, or rape. The captions and names might change, but the story is always the same. Somewhere in the quagmire of sin a man is lost in the pit of shame.

Perhaps you can relate to some of the headlines from days gone by. Your sins might not be as wild or crass, but your shame is just as heavy as any other man's. Before you wallow in that pit any longer, let's take a better look at the pathway of shame.

1.  Shame leads to sequential sin. What was once exciting now requires more to satisfy an insatiable hunger. (Romans 1:21–32)
2.  Shame leads to silence. Now in the grips of the enemy's talons, the whispering accusations in your mind silence the lips. (Revelation 12:10b)
3.  Shame leads to seclusion. With the enemy's accusations whirling in your head, the fear of condemnation counsels for seclusion. (Genesis 3:8)

4.  Shame leads to severance. Once sin is exposed by the light of truth, society and our Sovereign King demand severance. (Genesis 4:16)

5.  Shame leads to the Judge's sentence. Unconfessed, habitual sin requires justice. A solo figure will listen as the Judge pronounces the sentence. (Galatians 6:7–8, Romans 1:32a)

Seems pretty dismal, doesn't it? But wait- there is hope. In the Bible, we are told the way out of this trap:

1.  Recognize the need for confession and repentance. (1 John 1:9)

2.  Receive freedom in God's truth. (Romans 8:1)

3.  Reconnect with a local body of Christ where others will hold you accountable to a godly lifestyle. (Titus 2:1–2, 6–8)

Take heart. Crawl out of shame's pit and walk into the light of God's love.

## Study the Playbook

**READ:** Luke 15:11–32; Acts 3:19; Revelation 2:5a

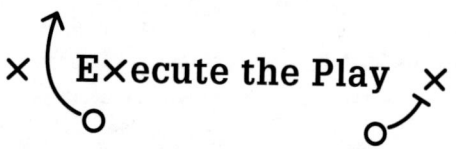

## Execute the Play

Sin is a cruel master. With the power of Christ, break that stranglehold! Admit to God all your sins. Turn away from those immoral behaviors and choose to live in truth and honor. Align yourself with mature and faithful Christians as you begin your journey of obedience.

# The Turk

**M**any might view him to be akin to the angel of death. Who or what is this Turk? He is the player the coaches have given the burdensome task of collecting those sad individuals who are being cut from the team. The Turk must find that hopeful player, oftentimes waking him from sleep in his room, and lead him down that long corridor to the room where the coach is waiting for him. The walk is usually silent, much like a sheep being led to the slaughter. What talk does get offered is usually small and strained.

Most of us can empathize with the player being cut. But some can really tune in to plight of The Turk. On the elementary playground, the other children see him as the goody-two-shoes, the teacher's pet. Not only do they avoid him like the plague, but they hurl the most offensive insults their young minds can conjure. On the corporate scene, middle management can often be seen as the snitch to the main office. Even though the duties and titles are legitimately given by the appropriate authorities, many of the other employ-

# MELANIE GARRETT

ees view those in middle management with contempt and distrust. Verbal daggers are thrown at their turned backs. At social gatherings, they often feel the chill of silent condemnation.

Here's the point. There will be times in our lives when those in authority are going to ask us to carry out an assignment or fill a position that is awkward or uncomfortable. Assuming that this requirement does not violate any biblical mandates, how does God expect us to respond? We are commanded to "submit … to every authority instituted among men" (1 Peter 2:13).

Why? We do it for the Lord's sake, so that all those who are watching (and believe me, we've got a pretty large audience) may "see *our* good deeds and glorify God" (1 Peter 2:12–13, italics mine).

So if we follow this teaching, will this make the outcome more palatable for us? Maybe, but probably not. What it will do is help us to keep our focus on God and His purposes, which in turn will remind us to draw strength from Him.

Let me encourage you. Whether you're The Turk or relegated to taking out the trash, be faithful to accomplish all that you've been directed to do. In the end, God will get the glory; and He will, in turn, exalt you (1 Peter 5:6).

## Study the Playbook

READ: Mark 10:45; Philippians 1:4; Matthew 20:1–16, 24:45–47

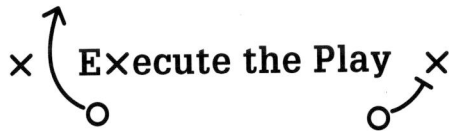

## Execute the Play

Today, determine that you will do your best, whatever task or assignment you're given. Have this mindset at work, home, in the community and at church. Remember, when done for the purpose of glorifying God and blessing others, all jobs are meaningful.

# When Your Best Isn't Good Enough

Super Bowl XXXIV, January 30, 2000, St. Louis Rams versus the Tennessee Titans, last play of the game. The Titans had the ball on the ten-yard line. Steve McNair threw a slant to Kevin Dyson, who caught it at the three. As he lunged for the goal line, Mike Jones tackled him on the one. The last six seconds on the game clock had expired. Kevin had left it all on the field, but it just wasn't good enough to win the Super Bowl. Dyson, along with the rest of his Titan teammates, walked off the field, dejected and defeated.

In corporate America, many hard working employees give 110 percent only to have their superiors pass them over with that well deserved promotion going to someone else. In the home, godly parents model a Christ-like life, teaching and training their children in the Lord. Yet, one child lets sin get a stranglehold in his life and deserts all that is good. In the marriage, despite every attempt one spouse makes to pursue developing a godly relationship , the other spouse views their marriage vows with contempt. Betrayal, divorce, and heartbreak are left in rebellion's wake.

In this sin-corrupted world there are going to be times, in spite of our most valiant efforts, that we find "it just isn't enough". What does God have to say? How does He want us, His children, to respond in such trying times?

First of all, it's crucial to remember that our significance is not wrapped up in our success. Our value is completely dependent upon God and our relationship with Him. He tells us, "I have loved you with an everlasting love" (Jeremiah 31:3).

Secondly, keep in mind that this world is not our home. Jesus said, "You do not belong to the world, but I have chosen you out of the world. That is why the world hates you" (John 15:19).

Ever since man revolted against a perfect God in Eden, the paradise God created for us here has become increasingly skewed and distorted. We must remember that this world is only a temporary stop in the journey to our eternal home in heaven.

Finally, we must avoid falling prey to despair. Paul wrote, "Let us not become weary in doing good …"

Though our best efforts seemingly have ended in defeat, we must continue to do what is right. Why? What's the pay off? Because "at the proper time we will reap a harvest if we do not give up" (Galatians 6:9)

Be encouraged, friend. Victory is waiting for us!

# Study the Playbook

**READ:** Psalm 73:26; 1 Peter 5:6–7;
Habakkuk 2:3; Philippians 1:6

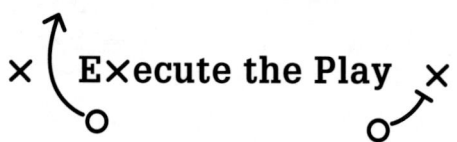

## Execute the Play

Your best may not have been enough, but God's best always is. Stop pushing the rewind button of your memories. Instead, come back to the present. Get up. Dust yourself off. Now tap into the strength God has given you and *live*.

_____

_____

_____

_____

_____

_____

_____

_____

_____

_____

# You Too?

**D**o you have one too? You know, a pre-game superstition? You want to know mine? It seems ridiculous when I talk about it out loud; but inside my head, it makes perfect sense. I love coffee as do many of you. So I have this little pre-game ritual. I make a fresh pot of coffee, choose any one of my team mugs, pour my java, and get ready for the game. Oh, one little detail: my "lucky" spoon. Can't remember where it came from, but it's the only one of its kind in my kitchen. And it fits perfectly in my hand. Stir in cream and sugar and I'm ready for kickoff. Sound silly? Well, try this. Last week, in all the excitement, I forgot my pre-game ritual. Yep, you guessed it. We lost. Today's game? No, I didn't forget this time. And, yes, we did win.

Do you still think it sounds silly? Probably so, but at least I'm in good company. Look around the league. Some players won't cut their hair when they're winning. Some won't shave. Some make the sign of the cross before kickoff. Others have to listen to their "lucky" song. Some players have a certain diet they eat on game day while others have a specific route to the stadium. The list goes on and on. But most players (and devout fans) find themselves caught up in superstition. Though the mind clearly dismisses the practice, the heart can't quite let go of the 'what-if' behind the rituals.

You might think this type of mentality only revolves around sports. Think again. How many people do you know who think they can win a ticket to heaven like this? You know, do just the right things, wear the Sunday best in clothing, say those specific words and *never ever* abandon the rituals. Is there any luck involved in getting into heaven? Jesus knew we would try to win a place inside those pearly gates. That's why over two thousand years ago He was so clear when He told His disciples, "I am the way, the truth, and the life. No one comes to the Father except through Me" (John 14:6).

No luck, no superstitious rituals, just simple truth and simple faith. Ready to give up your pre-game rituals? I'm not sure I'm ready to give up my "lucky" spoon. But eternity? Are you willing to leave your destination up to superstition or rituals? Me? No thanks, I think I'll pass that up for the Truth.

## Study the Playbook

**READ:** Romans 3:10, 20;
Isaiah 57:13, 64:6; Ephesians 2:8–10

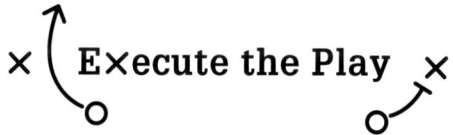

## Execute the Play

Stop trying to earn, win or "luck" your way into Heaven. Instead, know for certain that the price for your admission has been paid in full. Research it for yourself. Look up the Bible verses about salvation and learn that Jesus is Who and What He has always claimed to be. Stop guessing. Make Him the Savior and Lord of your life today!

# 24/7

"Football. Twenty-four-seven." It's one of the promotional ads for the NFL Network. If you love the game, you've gotta love this. Every day, every show- it's all about football. The programming offers a good deal of variety. Some shows give us current news throughout the league. Others give us a personal glimpse into the player, his past and current life and his passions. A favorite for many is the replay of the top games from that week. And during the off-season, there is a glut of classic games from the past, both long ago and recent. If you're like me, it is tough to pry yourself away from the remote, which seems frozen to the NFL Network. So many of us dedicate such commitment to the game that they gave football its own television network!

"Football. Twenty-four-seven." What makes this promo so appealing? Perhaps it's because it taps into an essential truth: we are created to live life full of passion and purpose. Think of the Christian life. What does God call us to do? Is it not to live for Him with the same or greater level of commitment and dedication as we do for a game? Let's dust off that Bible and discover the 24/7 mentality God calls His children to live out:

1. We are to live for Him in such a way that all people come to know Him as their Savior. "Let your light shine before men, that they may see your good deeds and praise your Father in heaven" (Matthew 5:16).

2. We are to live our faith before our children so that it teaches them about a real and loving God. "These commandments that I give you today are to be upon your hearts. Impress them on your children. Talk about them when you sit at home and when you walk along the road, when you lie down and when you get up" (Deuteronomy 6:6–7).

3. We are to: "pray, continually" (1 Thessalonians 5:17).

4. We are to be students of the Word. "Do your best to present yourself to God as one approved, a workman who does not need to be ashamed and who correctly handles the Word of Truth" (2 Timothy 2:15).

All of these indicate that the way we live for Christ should be so fervent that it is compelling. In a nutshell, our life should be, "Christ. Twenty-four-seven."

## Study the Playbook

**READ:** Philippians 1:27, 2:14–15; 1 John 2:3–6; Matthew 22:37–39

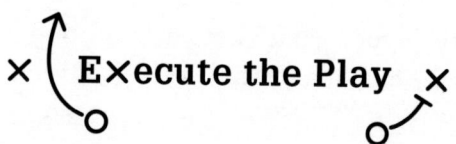

## Execute the Play

Be who you say you are. Read. Study. Pray.
Worship. Glorify. Fellowship. Serve. Witness.
Love. Forgive. Live for Christ: 24/7!

## listen|imagine|view|experience

### AUDIO BOOK DOWNLOAD INCLUDED WITH THIS BOOK!

In your hands you hold a complete digital entertainment package. In addition to the paper version, you receive a free download of the audio version of this book. Simply use the code listed below when visiting our website. Once downloaded to your computer, you can listen to the book through your computer's speakers, burn it to an audio CD or save the file to your portable music device (such as Apple's popular iPod) and listen on the go!

How to get your free audio book digital download:

1. Visit www.tatepublishing.com and click on the e|LIVE logo on the home page.
2. Enter the following coupon code:
   00c1-eb14-1400-d58e-2632-c73d-515a-1c70
3. Download the audio book from your e|LIVE digital locker and begin enjoying your new digital entertainment package today!